1991

Social Support Systems in Practice

W9-ACL-935

Maguire, Lambert.
Social support systems in prac

3 0301 00067688 8

A Generalist Approach

Lambert Maguire

National Association of Social Workers
Silver Spring, MD 20910

LIBRARY
College of St. Francis
JOLIET, ILLINOIS

NASW PRESS

Barbara W. White, ACSW, *President*
Mark G. Battle, ACSW, *Executive Director*

© 1991 by the NASW Press

All rights reserved. No part of this book may be reproduced or transmitted in any form or by any means, electronic or mechanical, including photocopying, recording, or by any information storage and retrieval system, without permission in writing from the publisher.

Library of Congress Cataloging-in-Publication Data

Maguire, Lambert.
    Social support systems in practice: a generalist approach/
Lambert Maguire.
    p. cm.
  Includes bibliographical references and index.
  ISBN 0-87101-189-1 (pbk. : alk. paper)
    1. Social case work—United States. 2. Social networks—United
States—Evaluation.   I. Title.
HV43.M26 1991   91-28008
361.3'2—dc20   CIP

Printed in the U.S.A.

Cover and interior design by Gary Mosteller, Arlington, Virginia.

361.32
M213

142,049

This book is dedicated to Barbara, Amy, and Mandy.

6.2.13

Contents

FOREWORD ix

ACKNOWLEDGMENTS xi

INTRODUCTION: SOCIAL SUPPORT SYSTEMS xiii

Resources Provided by Social Support xv
Organization of the Book xix
References xx

1. DEFINING SOCIAL SUPPORT AND MENTAL HEALTH 1

Analyzing Social Support 2
Defining the Client's Social Support System 5
Development of the Definition of Mental Health 10
Current Research and Epidemiological Studies 14
Questions 18
References 19

2. SOCIAL SUPPORT SYSTEM INTERVENTION: THEORY AND PRACTICE 21

The Social Support System Model 22
Social Support System Interventions: The Model, Theory, Empirical Base, and Values 23
Three Major Types of Intervention 26
The Five Stages of System Development 33
Problems and Limitations 38
Why Social Support Intervention Should Be Used 41
Helping the Natural Process Work 45
Questions 46
References 47

3. WORKING WITH DEPRESSED INDIVIDUALS 51

Problems in Using Social Support 51
Treating Depressed Individuals 57
Questions 69
References 69

4. MARRIAGE AND SOCIAL SUPPORT   71

Marriage and the Mental Health of Men and Women   71
Key Questions and Their Use in Marital Work   84
Questions   95
References   96

5. THE FAMILY AS A SOCIAL SUPPORT SYSTEM   98

The Family, Health, and Mental Health   98
Helping the Family Function as a Social   108
  Support System
Contemporary Changes in Family Structure   111
NASW's "Family Support Principles"   121
Questions   122
References   123

6. SOCIAL SUPPORT SYSTEMS IN THE LIFE STAGES   125

Childhood   125
Adolescence   131
Adulthood   137
The Elderly   146
Personal Retrospective of Life Crises Exercise   151
References   152

7. APPLICATIONS OF SOCIAL SUPPORT SYSTEMS: 154
   PAST, PRESENT, AND FUTURE

Past and Present Applications   154
Future Applications   158
AIDS   171
Questions   175
References   176

INDEX   179

ABOUT THE AUTHOR   187

Case Examples

Balancing Support and Separateness   42

The Motorcycle Man   57

The Reversible Couple   64

Self-blame and Self-esteem   78

Infidelity and Its Rewards   81

Defining the Problem   85

Establishing Boundaries and Ownership   87

Developing a Plan   92

Mike's Great Expectations   103

The Newly Reconstituted Family   118

Jimmy's Need for Attention   129

Jenny, the Perfect Teen   133

The Secretary   143

Mary, Mother without a Role   148

Schizophrenics and Social Support   162

Mildred: Homeless and Lost in the System   169

Foreword

It is most appropriate that the NASW Press publish *Social Support Systems in Practice: A Generalist Approach* for a number of reasons. Social work is a practice profession, and the National Association of Social Workers (NASW), as the primary organization representing social work practitioners, assumes an obligation to provide tools to help them improve their practice. This book answers the need for a good text for general social work practice.

As social workers, we take a person-in-environment perspective that views clients as part of an environmental system. We look at people where they live in their arena of family, friends, and other networks, and we help them cope with their problems in that context. Lambert Maguire has written a practical guide to using these natural support systems to augment interventions by social workers and other human services professionals. Maguire demonstrates, through case studies and practice guidelines, how clients can take charge of their own destiny more effectively when they connect to and make use of their social support systems.

NASW has placed considerable emphasis on families, which we define as any collection of individuals who define themselves as family and who take on the responsibilities and functions generally considered necessary for healthy family life. "Strengthening Families" was the association's theme for the 1990–91 public service campaign, and we are following that with "Global Family Ties" for the 1992 campaign. *Social Support Systems* offers valuable guidelines for working with individuals and family members in contemporary families.

Practitioners will find this book helpful in their practice. In addition, the book is a valuable text for use in schools of social work, particularly in baccalaureate programs. This connection, too, is in line with NASW priorities as we seek new ways to make the association's program more useful to baccalaureate practitioners.

For general practice information and as a clear, practical guide to the theory and application of social work interventions, we recommend *Social Support Systems in Practice: A Generalist Approach.*

Barbara W. White, PhD, ACSW
NASW President

Mark G. Battle, ACSW
NASW Executive Director

Acknowledgments

I would like to thank my good friend Tony Tripodi for his encouragement and support throughout the writing of this book. A special thanks goes to Mercedes McBride, who typed the many drafts of the manuscript. Thanks also go to Dean David Epperson, who consistently supports his faculty and who sets the tone for the exceptionally friendly and nurturing atmosphere that exists here at Pitt. Finally, I would like to thank Lisa Braxton and Nancy Winchester of the National Association of Social Workers and Dorothy Sawicki for their help and suggestions on the manuscript.

Introduction

Social Support Systems

This book for social work practitioners is designed to be a practical guide to the use of social support systems. A support system, according to Caplan (1974), one of the early pioneers in the field, "implies an enduring pattern of continuous or intermittent ties that play a significant part in maintaining the psychological and physical integrity of the individual over time" (p. 7). Whittaker and Garbarino (1983) described a social support network as "a set of interconnected relationships among a group of people that provides enduring patterns of nurturance (in any or all forms) and provides contingent reinforcement for efforts to cope with life on a day to day basis" (p. 5).

In these and other definitions can be found certain commonly accepted notions about the nature and purpose of social support systems. They are, for instance, types of relationships among defined sets of people; they are enduring, as families and good friendships are; and they provide encouragement, caring, and direction to individuals, particularly to those in need.

How much, from a practical standpoint, can social support systems help social workers on a day-to-day basis deal with the demanding problems presented by their clients? The answer is that social support systems, when adequately understood and appropriately focused, can be used very effectively by social workers and other health and mental health professionals in direct, daily practice to help those whose lives have been disrupted in some way that has resulted in the loss of close personal ties.

Most clients first come to see social workers because of stressful situations that involve the actual, potential, or feared loss of love, affection, or support from someone. Whether the clients are depressed divorcées, unemployed individuals, school dropouts, children whose parents cannot or do not show them affection in appropriate ways, teenagers who have no peer groups, or elderly clients whose loved ones have died, each has suffered losses in his or her social support system. Thus, logic suggests that the most practical point of intervention for them is at the level of their own immediate social support systems or networks.

In recent years, many social workers have recognized the need for social support to protect people from the effects of stress and to help them cope better. Historically, the basic unit of support for most people, adults as well as children, has been their families, because marriages and families can provide the strong, intimate bonds that people need. Such intimate relationships ideally allow people to explore their innermost thoughts, hopes, and fears. Not only are the expression and communication of these concerns essential for finding purpose and meaning in life, but people also need to share their thoughts in order to validate them or to change their feelings, behaviors, or perceptions. Without intimate relationships to provide such an outlet, people may become increasingly isolated or even deviant in their feelings and actions. Without a basic familial support system, individuals frequently succumb to the effects of the stresses and traumas of modern-day living.

Caplan (1974) identified three major forms of assistance operating in social support systems. First, the significant others help the individual to use his or her own psychological resources and overcome difficulties, empowering the person thus supported to deal with the causes of the stress. Second, the system shares in such tasks as cleaning house, paying bills, or preparing meals to limit the amount of stress on the overburdened individual and to clearly show concern and caring. Third, social support systems give extra resources, such as guidance, money, material, or skills, to help the individual handle difficult situations better.

House (1981) noted three purposes that social support systems serve. First, less desirable influences are crowded out as support-iveness increases, so negatively stressful situations and stimuli become less dominating as positive interaction and types of help grow. Second, general health improves as individuals begin to take better care of themselves under the influence of caring support or become more aware of their realistic roles in solving their problems. Finally, social support serves as a buffer against the effects of stress, thus protecting people from such common psychological overreactions as self-blame and guilt and from physical reactions such as lethargy, sleeping or eating disorders related to depression, or abuse of alcohol or other drugs.

With regard to health, epidemiological research indicates that four mechanisms of social support may explain the lowering of mortality rates as the use of social support systems and networks expands. These mechanisms are as follows: (1) providing care directly to individuals; (2) advising or supporting individuals in their efforts to seek appropriate self-care or medical attention; (3) modeling healthy self-care for these individuals, encouraging them to avoid unhealthy or high-risk behaviors; and (4) providing psychosocial interaction, which is believed to help general immunity to disease (Berkman, 1985).

Resources Provided by Social Support

By analyzing social support in terms of its practical components, one can see that it provides at least five resources, which are discussed below: (1) a sense of self; (2) encouragement and positive feedback; (3) protection against stress; (4) knowledge, skills, and resources; and (5) socialization opportunities.

A Sense of Self

Many clients of social workers have difficulty with individuality. They have a poor sense of who they are or what they want. Through enmeshment, symbiosis, overidentification, or codependency, they have lost a meaningful sense of themselves. Although the dynamics of this loss may differ in each of those cases, the result is the same: the client defines himself or herself in relation to others—not as a unique, self-responsible, autonomous human being; the line between "self" and "other" is blurred. It is often only through a healthy involvement with a supportive social system that individuals can learn or relearn about themselves.

Social support offers the interactional environment that lets people appreciate their uniqueness. The members of a social support system are anchored around the individual, permitting that person to develop an awareness of his or her own autonomous and unique existence as a thinking, feeling human being. Perhaps surprisingly, the best way for those in a social support system to help in this regard is to do nothing but listen. People dealing with less severe emotional problems feel that they are best helped by going to friends or relatives and "just talking about it" (Maguire & Martz, in press). They neither want nor need mental health professionals to intervene or to "do something." Empathic, supportive social workers probably tap into this perspective best, because they recognize that people need to be trusted to figure out their own best paths. They recognize that when people are simply encouraged through nonjudgmental, genuine acceptance to understand themselves, they ultimately come, without direction, to solutions compatible with their own best interests. Thus, reflective listening and empathy are methods social workers can use in early phases of treatment as they begin to develop social supports to help people view their concerns introspectively, as individuals with ultimate responsibility for their own fates.

Encouragement and Positive Feedback

People constantly evaluate themselves in light of what others say and do. They need to know that they are valued and needed. Many clients come for help with a damaged, traumatized sense of their own self-worth. Those who have been abandoned, neglected, or in some other way hurt and devalued by others invariably begin to question their own worth, wondering how, if others care so little for them, they can justify caring for themselves. By contrast, a positively oriented social support system provides people feedback that they have worth and are valued. This in turn can give them the confidence to change behavior that had been based on assumptions that they had little or nothing to offer others.

A helping professional can use social support systems to strengthen this process by serving as a role model for behavior that reinforces the client's positive and constructive attitudes and behaviors. For instance, when talking with family, friends, or co-workers of the client, the professional can be a role model by focusing on the client's ability with children or by pointing out his or her kindness. Just as social systems can become negative in their orientation toward and perceptions of an individual (for example, the family and friends of a chronically depressed client or an alcoholic), so too can they eventually be turned around to be supportive (as the family and friends of a highly valued community leader, respected teacher, or caring member of the clergy would be).

Protection against Stress

Evidence suggests that social support is essentially a protective mechanism. Research indicates that when a stressful situation such as the loss of a job, a divorce, the death of a spouse, or a major medical problem develops, people with strong social support systems handle the stressor more successfully. This holds true regardless of what category people happen to be in—pregnant women who are more likely to deliver infants successfully without medical complications (Nuckolls, Cassel, & Kaplan, 1972), men who stay physically and mentally healthy despite job loss (Gore, 1978), or children whose parents were recently divorced but who received social support from peers at school (Kalter, Schaefer, Lesowitz, Alpern, & Kickar, 1988).

Professionals in mental health and social services can build this protective buffer against stress by making family, friends, and other members of the system well aware that they are important to the client and by pointing out to them how helpful they can be. Family and friends who at first may be only peripherally involved with the client can become a more vital part of the process by getting this sort of positive feedback themselves. Their sense of altruism and of being caring people can be encouraged so that a stronger involvement with the client is developed. Family and friends sometimes need to be reminded that their occasional words of support or encouragement or simply their willingness to listen can be immeasurably helpful to the client. They may also need to have it explained to them that the success of so many social support endeavors really depends on some very basic human behavior, such as showing the same level of caring, encouragement, and support that any good friend would offer. It will help if they realize that the essence of helping professions in many ways is simply showing those qualities of humanity that are most admired in caring people—genuine concern and empathy for others.

Knowledge, Skills, and Resources

Social support systems can help with specific problems by providing useful information—for example, where to go for a job or money, or how to approach an alienated friend or relative. Members of a caring social support system also give individuals who need them the tools to rebuild their lives. Such help can come from an uncle who gives a client a job, an aunt who sensitively confronts the client with his or her maladaptive behavior, or even another client who perhaps belongs to the same self-help group.

Self-help groups are useful components of social support systems, particularly as providers of knowledge, skills, and resources. In working with a particular client, mental health and social service professionals often find their best allies in other clients who have lived through the same trauma, be it cancer, the problems of adjusting to divorce, the effects of incest, or the ongoing battle of alcoholics for sobriety. The credibility of these fellow sufferers tends to be high among clients in need of social support, and at times they can provide information that the professional cannot. For instance, social workers in hospital systems would be ill-advised to suggest to members of a support group for women who have had mastectomies that they should avoid certain physicians or seek out certain specialists. However, within such support groups there is often discussion of the abilities and sensibilities of other professionals within the system. Similarly, clients with orthopedic problems often need limbs or other expensive devices that may require very particular skills to produce. The professional might not know that Joe, the shoe repairman at the shop on Second Street, is actually much more skilled than the hospital's staff at making lifts for shoes, or that he charges 50 percent less. Discussions along these lines are often extremely useful for clients not only because of the information itself, but also because such altruistic caring and self-help efforts considerably enhance each member's sense of self-worth.

The types of help that members of a cancer support group received are typical for other such groups. The members indicated that the most valuable benefit from their participation involved emotional support, caring, understanding, hope, or friendship (33 percent), followed by the ability to compare themselves with others suffering the same malady (23 percent), and then the ability to obtain specific information about medical issues (Taylor, Falke, Mazel, & Hilsberg, 1988).

Socialization Opportunities

Many clients of social workers have poor social skills. For some, this may be a temporary setback, reflecting their withdrawal as a result of a divorce, a recent health problem, or a blow to their self-esteem from losing a job. Others have had poor social skills since early childhood for any of a variety of social, psychological, or even genetic or physiological reasons. Whatever the cause, interaction with others can enhance self-worth and, in addition to providing the type of specific help described above, it also breaks a cycle of isolation. It may allow a client with poor social skills to become involved in relationships rather than continuing to cut off from other people. For some clients, nearly any social activity is positive. A church service, athletic event, or bingo game, preferably with a friend or relative, can be that significant first step in the right direction. The habit of cutting out social contacts needs to be counteracted with encouragement to meet new friends and to reestablish old relationships.

Socialization generally involves a series of discussions about the client's past relationships and about what those relationships meant and how they helped. This process is enhanced from the outset when the professional has the client diagram or describe his or her social support system. From this, discussions inevitably develop that lead the client to reconsider the meaning and utility of past and future relationships. Clients who have responded to stress and a deflated self-image by cutting off social ties can usually see that this is hurting them and that the best way to turn their problem around may be to reengage with others who care about them and for whom they care.

Organization of the Book

This practical guide to the use of social support systems examines the variety of ways in which social work practitioners can organize family, friends, and fellow professionals into therapeutic, rehabilitative, or preventive units of help for clients.

The book describes three different approaches to such social support systems: network intervention, case management, and social support system development. However, a generalist orientation is recommended. Rather than making precise distinctions that differentiate between often subtle nuances to distinguish one approach from another, the book takes a broader approach. By "generalist" is meant that it advocates broad-based application of social support system utilization to a variety of psychosocial problems.

Social workers are often required to be generalists in their practices, and this volume attempts to help them meet that need. The clients of social workers are individuals, families, groups, and communities, with needs emanating from myriad psychological, social, political, economic, developmental, racial, and gender-based biases and problems. The appropriate therapeutic responses must therefore be sufficiently wide to meet these diverse demands.

Because the book is designed to be a practical guide for social work practitioners in their use of social support systems, it is necessary to clarify the terms used. The first chapter thus looks in some depth at social support and mental health, before chapter 2 turns to social support system intervention and describes the three categories of intervention that the book concentrates on—system development, case management, and network intervention. Chapter 3 focuses on the practical use of social support systems with depressed clients while addressing several problems social workers can anticipate. Marriage is examined as a social support system in chapter 4, which also discusses gender issues and a variety of social and economic forces that need to be considered in working with clients. Families, children and extended family are addressed in chapter 5, with special attention to the "Family Support Principles" of the National Association of Social Workers. Chapter 6 looks at life cycles and the differing needs of individuals and families from infancy to old age. Finally, in chapter 7, a brief historical summary of social support systems is followed by a discussion of present and likely future applications, particularly for the long-term mentally ill, those affected by chronic poverty, and those with AIDS.

References

Berkman, L. F. (1985). The relationship of social networks and social support to morbidity and mortality. In S. Cohen & S. L. Syme (Eds.), *Social support and health*. Orlando, FL: Academic Press.

Caplan, G. (1974). *Support systems and community mental health: Lectures on concept development*. New York: Behavioral Publications.

Gore, S. (1978). The effect of social support in moderating the health consequences of unemployment. *Journal of Health and Social Behavior, 19*, 157–165.

House, J. (1981). *Work, stress and social support*. Reading, MA: Addison-Wesley.

Kalter, N., Schaefer, M., Lesowitz, M., Alpern, P., & Kickar, J. (1988). School-based support groups for children of divorce: A model of brief intervention. In B. J. Gottlieb (Ed.), *Marshalling social support: Formats, processes and effects* (pp. 165–186). Newbury Park, CA: Sage.

Maguire, L., & Martz, P. (in press). Youth face unemployment: An international comparison. In J. Cunningham & P. Martz (Eds.), *Family matters*. Pittsburgh: University of Pittsburgh Press.

Nuckolls, K. B., Cassel, J., & Kaplan, B. H. (1972). Psychosocial assets, life crises, and the prognosis of pregnancy. *American Journal of Epidemiology, 95*, 431–444.

Taylor, S. E., Falke, R. L., Mazel, R. M., & Hilsberg, B. L. (1988). Sources of satisfaction and dissatisfaction among members of cancer support groups. In B. J. Gottlieb (Ed.), *Marshalling social support: Formats, processes and effects* (pp. 187–208). Newbury Park, CA: Sage.

Whittaker, J. K., & Garbarino, J. (1983). *Social support networks: Informal helping in the human services*. New York: Aldine.

Chapter 1

Defining Social Support and Mental Health

Like many a religious convert, I once experienced a conversion as a result of a traumatic experience. It came about this way. My first assignment as a young social worker was at the Community Mental Health Program on the Pine Ridge Indian Reservation in South Dakota. With all the confidence that only the young and untested are privileged to enjoy, I undertook my work with the Oglala Sioux knowing that I had been well educated in psychodynamic and psychosocial theory, the task-centered approach, some problem-solving techniques, and other techniques such as uncovering the unconscious. I also had some empathic skills to help clients formulate their concerns more precisely. (Of course all of these theories, techniques, and skills are based on the client's capacity to verbalize psychological concerns after sufficient introspection.) I was not the least prepared for what I encountered.

The Sioux are a fiercely proud, independent, and intelligent people who trust and rely on their own close family and friends for any and all kinds of help. For perfectly understandable historical reasons, they do not trust most white people, even well-intentioned social workers. Furthermore, they do not dwell on analyzing reasons for their behavior, and even when they do, they do not talk about them. Complaining or blaming other people or life's circumstances is not looked upon with admiration by them, and it is generally in that light that they perceived therapeutic interventions. So I spent my first year at Pine Ridge trying to get my clients to "open up," or to "break through their resistance," or to "develop a therapeutic relationship," or even to define their problems and tasks clearly—all with relatively little success.

1

By the second of my three years at the Pine Ridge Reservation, two factors were becoming apparent, which accounted in large part for my "conversion" from traditional and rather psychodynamically oriented therapist to social support interventionist. First, there were many resources available in that community, but none of the really powerful resources were within the formal or professional system. Second, the thousands of people we did not see in the Community Mental Health Program were frequently under the same stresses and strains as the people we did see. It became apparent to me that most people were getting help either from their family members—usually through one of the major six or seven *tiospayes,* or extended families—or from various community leaders or tribal elders.

In other words, the Oglala Sioux were being helped by using their own social support systems of family and friends. And that, of course, is the theme of this book—helping people through the use of social support systems. Specifically, it is about how social work practitioners can help vastly diverse clients suffering from many different problems—but having in common some disruption of their lives involving the loss of close personal ties—to discover, to foster, and to use this natural resource of social support systems.

Analyzing Social Support

Social support has become focal to social work practice. Essentially the term refers to positive interactions in a person's social system, that is, in the general social environment or ecology within which that person lives. This environment is made up of an informal system including family, friends, colleagues at work or school, and neighbors, and a formal system of helpers including social workers, doctors, lawyers, clergy, and other professionals. In recent years, social workers and other helping professionals have been studying these systems so that they can establish more clearly the most effective and efficient means of using them to help people deal with a variety of psychosocial problems. In many instances the study of these systems involves a rather detailed quantitative or methodologically precise analysis of the system—in which case it is more accurate to speak of what is called a social network. The notion of a network, which originated for social scientists with some early anthropologists (Bott, 1971; Fischer, 1982), is an analytic approach by which the nature, type, frequency, density, range, and certain qualitative characteristics of an individual's social system are all measured and described for a defined set of people (Burt & Minor, 1983).

The overlap and occasional substitution of the terms social network and social support system for one another are understandable but technically inaccurate. A social support system usually connotes positive things: help, guidance, and caring provided by family members, friends, professionals, and others. Although a network may operate in either positive or negative ways, the term as used in analytic studies is essentially neutral. That is, a social network acting in a positive way would be an extended family that rallies around a young mother whose child is ill. A network with negative effects would be the social network of many alcoholics, which excludes and rejects abstinent members. But strictly speaking, the neutral sense is the most accurate: that is, the social network used as a method of analysis to help us understand precisely how and why people affect each other through various types of social exchanges or in the process of giving and taking resources from each other. For instance, Fischer (1982) studied the migration patterns of Africans as they moved from small rural villages to cities. Members from the same tribe would usually end up congregating in a certain city neighborhood because of a friend or cousin who had moved there and told others in his or her network. Fischer examined the patterns of influence and communication. Bott (1971) used a similar network analytic approach in examining the influence of in-laws on young married couples in suburban London. Through her analyses, she could trace the effects of in-laws on the marriage and on other aspects of family dynamics for these couples.

These and other studies in social network analysis simply attempt to describe, often in quantitative terms, the impact that people have on each other. So that we can learn how best to intervene to make social networks become social support systems, we must understand how the networks work.

There has been rapid growth in the literature which suggests that social support can in some way affect mental health and social functioning and that social support can be developed for clients. In fact, an annotated bibliography describing research and publications on mental health issues and social networks from 1966 to 1982 lists 1,340 citations (Biegel, McCardle, & Mendelson, 1985). The growth in this area has been so phenomenal that the bibliography was updated for 1983 to 1987 (Biegel, Farkas, Abell, Goodin, & Friendman, 1989).

It seems that social workers and others have become very aware that social support does indeed significantly affect mental health. However, there are difficulties with terminology in this area also. There is much confusion in the field because both *social support* and *mental health* mean many things to many people. We have already described in general some of the various aspects of the term social support. With regard to mental health, although one might assume that all those using the term are referring to the same concept, doing research in this area soon reveals that it has many different meanings.

To some, mental health is the absence of psychopathology or of any psychiatric disorder as defined in the *Diagnostic and Statistical Manual of Mental Disorders, Third Edition—Revised* (American Psychiatric Association, 1987). In other words, if a person cannot be labeled by terminology from the manual, he or she is mentally healthy.

Another viewpoint, which is preferred by those who do large studies using secondary data, sees improved mental health as being reflected in lower recidivism rates by individuals to psychiatric hospitals, increased employment in certain "at-risk" populations, higher salaries for those populations, maintenance of the family unit, lower incidence of institutionalization of any sort, or a decrease in the numbers of people "at risk" who are not on welfare.

Still others see mental health more philosophically, as Carl Rogers did. To them it is more an interior condition of being in touch with one's feelings and acting and perceiving oneself accordingly. For them, mental health means a feeling of wholeness and the ability not to judge oneself or others in strictly right-or-wrong, black-or-white terms. Many social services and mental health professionals combine these ideas and generally subscribe to an interactional model of mental health as being evident when one performs his or her role functions adequately and with some sense of satisfaction while enjoying a positive self-image and keeping up social relations.

How we define these terms operationally in clinical social work practice is not a purely heuristic exercise because, although we may rarely be consciously aware of it, from the moment a client walks in the door of a social agency, social workers begin the process of defining and deciding what social support and mental health are for this person. The problem for many professionals in practice today is that, with only a rough, general understanding of what they really mean by these terms, the initial assessment or database is inevitably imprecise and, consequently, intervention in terms of the ultimate goals of mental health or social functioning is also unclear. Thus, social workers need to define social support and mental health operationally so that their interventions, which are increasingly centered on these terms, can achieve greater efficiency based on the greater clarity of purpose that would result from precise definitions.

Defining the Client's Social Support System

Upon first seeing a client, the social worker immediately begins identifying the presenting problem and its history, and the worker must also operationally define that particular client's social support system. Taking as the operational definition of a mentally healthy individual "one who interacts well in a healthy, balanced social support system" requires information on the following categories, which go beyond standard demographics and diagnosis:

- Marital status
- Family composition in household
- Number and age of siblings, and frequency and type of contact
- Current parental involvement
- Employment status
- Neighborhood involvement
- Membership in organizations such as religious or church groups, self-help groups, sororities or fraternal organizations, unions, ethnic clubs, social clubs, political groups or causes, sports or athletic teams, parent groups or organizations, neighborhood "institutions" or "hangouts" such as bars or street corners.

The process of defining the client's social support system can be informal and generally developed during the first few sessions. Gathering the information in this way not only adds depth and meaning to the data, but it also helps the worker develop rapport with the client. The social worker can also use a more precise instrument for obtaining the same information, but many avoid using a formal instrument initially so as not to appear overly bureaucratic or insensitive.

A formal instrument, such as those discussed next, is rarely, if ever, used at the initial sessions in clinical work (as opposed to when it is used for research), because clients often cannot relate to it, and it may have the effect of distancing them from the social worker. Because so many clients lack social supports defined in terms of family, friends, and others, its use could also inadvertently trigger an even greater sense of despair in an already depressed or socially isolated person. Using it too early often leads to rejection of treatment.

If after the initial sessions the worker wants to define social support in a more precise and efficient manner, however, he or she might use some variation of the method shown in Figure 1-1, followed up with the use of the Personal Networking Assessment Instrument (Figure 1-2) (Maguire, 1983). To form the diagram, the worker draws three concentric circles. The client's name is placed in the middle. The outer circles are cut into three pie-shaped wedges, labeled *"Friends," "Family,"* and *"Other"* (the latter would include professionals, clergy, groups, and so forth).

Clients are asked to describe their social support network by writing in the names or initials of those to whom they feel closest. The results are sometimes surprising, as was the case with the diagram shown in Figure 1-3, which was completed by a depressed 12-year-old boy named Jim at the beginning of his third session.

Jim surprised the social worker by his network diagram in two ways. First, Jim's mother, a very depressed, anxious divorcée with three children, brought her son to the social worker because she felt that he had no friends, was depressed, and was possibly suicidal. Jim's diagram, however, indicated that he had a great many friends compared to other 12-year-old boys. He was also a leader of his Boy Scout troop and a member of a church group and a baseball team. So, the first surprise was that Jim was not at all a social isolate.

Second, the diagram showed that Jim's mother and one brother were close to him but that his father and the other brother were distant and estranged. This information from the diagram was helpful inasmuch as the social worker's previous, superficial discussions with Jim about his father and other siblings had not sufficiently alerted her to some real anger at his father, who had left the family for another

Figure 1-1.
Diagram for defining the client's social support network.

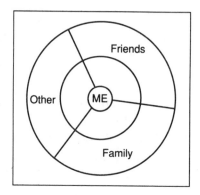

Name, Address, and Telephone #	Relationship (Relative, Friend, Neighbor, Work, Professional, Helper or Other)	Willingness to Help (High, Medium, Low)	Capabilities Social/ Emotional (briefly comment)	Resources Material/ Contacts (briefly comment)	Frequency of Contact (Daily, Weekly, Biweekly, Monthly, Less)	Duration of Friendship (Month, 6 Mos., Year, 1-5 Years, Longer)	Intensity (Direction and Degree of Affection and Comfort — briefly comment)
1.							
2.							
3.							
4.							
5.							

Figure 1-2. Personal Networking Assessment Instrument (*Source:* Maguire, 1983, p. 78).

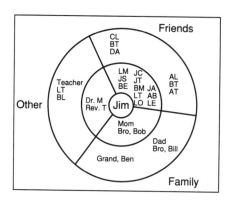

Figure 1-3.
Diagram as completed by
12-year-old client Jim.

woman, or to this boy's jealousy of an older brother with whom the father maintained a close personal relationship.

Jim's diagram also showed that he had developed a rather unusual split in his social network. As the social worker discussed the diagram with him, Jim explained that he felt unhappy at home but less so at school and with his friends. His mother was so depressed and angry at his father that Jim also felt her depression at home, and, although he himself felt abandoned by and angry at his father, some of this was out of his need for approval from his mother. (He explained that his mother was very hurt if he said anything positive about his father.) Jim's father, according to subsequent interviews, turned out to be a rather good and caring, if immature and irresponsible, man. Jim therefore presented at home as being depressed, and indeed he was; but in other social situations he was a reasonably healthy, adjusted boy.

The social worker worked closely with Jim and his mother to get them to separate some of their feelings from each other while providing help and support. The mother recognized that Jim was strongly affected by her feelings toward her ex-husband, so she sought further help on an individual basis and let Jim know that his feelings for his father, positive as well as negative, were all right and that he did not have to feel the same way she did.

In the preceding example, diagramming permitted the clear analysis of the social network that proved diagnostically necessary. The example also points out the difference in being supportive and being enmeshed, or too strongly identified with another person. By getting clients to draw these diagrams relatively early in the intervention, the social worker accomplishes three things:

1. *Better assessment.* Social networks allow interpersonal dynamics to be diagnosed clearly and concisely, which in turn leads to better assessment and diagnosis of what is

actually happening in the person's social system. Without this structure, many issues can be missed.

2. *Greater client awareness.* In drawing their own diagrams, clients must examine very clearly their feelings and attitudes about family, friends, and others. They begin to think in terms of social support and helpful interactions and become profoundly aware of how others affect them.

3. *The beginning of strategic thinking.* Clients cannot diagram their entire social system without beginning to see not only how it affects them, but also what they can or cannot do to help themselves. As the social worker and the client discuss, for example, the effects of a sibling's bitter criticisms or an aunt's constant praise and encouragement, the groundwork for change is being strongly and clearly developed.

Another method of formally analyzing the social support system is to use the network diagram followed up with a series of specific questions. Typically this is done informally over the period of the first few sessions, but the social worker may choose to collect these data in a thorough fashion initially, particularly in order to evaluate the client's progress. Thus, the following questions could be gradually and informally asked as an alternative to the more formal personal networking assessment instrument:

A. What is this person's relationship to you (for example, cousin, aunt, neighbor, co-worker, teacher)? _____

B. How long have you known this person?_____months or _____ years

C. How often do you have contact with this person by telephone or in person? (Choose one)
   _____ times per week
   _____ times per month
   _____ times per year
   _____ other

D. Briefly describe what you receive from this person (for example, advice, money, a "shoulder to cry on")._____
   _____
   _____

E. What do you think this person receives in return from you?
   _____
   _____
   _____

Traditionally trained mental health professionals who have historically focused more on purely intrapsychic phenomena or, in the case of some psychiatrists, on neurological and biochemical aspects of mental illness, have now discovered what staff in social service agencies and community mental health centers have known for many years: that social support systems can and must be carefully analyzed and understood before any clinical intervention can proceed. Just as medical science is making great strides in helping in the understanding of the biochemical and genetic forces in the causes and cures of social/emotional problems and mental illness, social workers in community or social agencies must continue to lead the way in understanding the social forces that have an impact on these same problems. As complex as these issues may be, clinicians cannot afford to be any less rigorous or demanding than neurologists or geneticists in their pursuit of efficient and humane interventions.

Development of the Definition of Mental Health

More than three centuries ago, the French philosopher Descartes developed a theory of the mind and body as two separate and distinct systems. This theory of dualism was the basis for modern medicine, especially in the West, where the body eventually came to be seen in a relatively mechanistic manner. Dualism served a highly useful purpose in that it forced philosophers as well as physicians to focus on the intricate and complex objects of their research and to practice with a useful and clear theoretical frame of reference. Even though technically incapable of being validated, these theoretical frames of reference provided a reasonable and constant foundation on which to base our understanding. Thus, physicians studied anatomy and chemistry, whereas philosophers and the precursors of social scientists examined behavior and its philosophical basis.

Years later, it was found in many European and colonial American "insane asylums" that by treating people humanely and supportively, the various "biles and humours" that caused the behavior were positively affected. Several model "hospitals" combined physical treatments, such as bloodletting, the use of leeches, and even calming baths, with kindness and rational discussions. This was in contrast to the more typical treatment of the mentally ill, which included isolating them and condoning brutal conditions—generally leading to extended, severe dysfunction away from family and friends.

At the turn of the 20th century, social workers and other "friendly helpers" worked with immigrant groups and the urban and rural poor by developing social supports. Even then it was clearly recognized that the best way to help these families and individuals, who were often dealing with acute reactions to change in their environments, was to get them linked up with others. As immigrant groups poured into the ports of Boston and New York or later found their way to Chicago, Cleveland, and St. Louis, these early social workers saw that what was needed was a sense of belonging and some help and support from others.

The most efficient and effective help was appropriately perceived as coming from those with whom these uprooted people shared certain common beliefs and cultures. Thus, social workers would link up the Irish with the clergy and Irish groups, and Jewish immigrants were put in contact with fellow Jews who were often from the same country. The synagogues, settlement houses, and churches that developed were not only religious institutions and cultural havens, but also resources for finding friends, getting jobs, and sharing joys and sorrows. Neighborhoods themselves were often homogeneous, and their residents protected and supported each other and their families. These social support systems were usually family-based but were closely connected to extended families of aunts, uncles, cousins and beyond, to in-laws and friends. Such neighborhoods were connected by people who identified with each other, sharing common backgrounds, interests, and orientations. They provided a psychologically healthy, supportive environment, nurtured by professionals who recognized the importance of support systems.

However, there was, and is today, a downside to this type of environment. The support that these family and ethnically based neighborhoods provided also supported a certain ethnocentric paranoia. Whereas pride in one's culture is healthy, for some this became exclusionary: "If you're not one of us, you're bad or a threat to us." Thus, the Little Italy and Polish Bush neighborhoods of Chicago, or the concentrations of Irish in South Boston, Jewish people in New York, black people in Harlem and other cities, and Mexican Americans in the barrios of Los Angeles all performed a negative function as well. Through the 1950s and even today, these tight ethnic neighborhoods disallowed and helped subvert any comfortable sharing and cross-fertilization of ideas and norms with those outside the neighborhood. In many instances there was a mutually agreed upon ghettoization—that is, the majority culture and the various ethnic and racial minorities in the neighborhood arranged themselves in tight networks of defense against other cultures. The benefits of social support seemed to outweigh the costs of racism and ethnocentrism, at least for some individuals if not for society at large.

The black population was particularly hurt by segregation, which began to decline after World War II and was forcibly changed during the Civil Rights movement of the 1960s. Black people and other minorities demanded and to some extent received the right to move to better neighborhoods and into better school systems and to apply for and receive better jobs and opportunities. This social integration undoubtedly helped the nation as a whole and black people in particular as they entered the mainstream American social system. However, even positive social change can have negative ramifications for minority groups. For instance, those in inner-city black ghettos have been particularly hurt in the past 10 to 20 years by societal racism compounded by the migration of middle-class blacks. Although education and civil rights have opened opportunities to some middle-class blacks, their moving from these communities has left behind the most disadvantaged (Wilson, 1987).

At the same time that this cultural history of the United States was developing, a concurrent series of events related to social work practice issues was taking place. In the 1920s, a new era began in social work agencies as well as in psychology. Although there has been some current debate about the extent to which social work embraced Freudian psychoanalysis, it is evident that many in the field welcomed it. The psychoanalytic approach adapted by the field gave social work the professional status it so desperately wanted and needed. It was revised and modified for the diverse populations served by social work, and it evolved eventually into the broad-based psychosocial approach of Florence Hollis. Since Hollis it has evolved even more, away from the intrapsychic and into the socioecological realm, as the field embraced Helen Harris Perlman's problem-solving approach, then Reid and Epstein's task-centered approach, and then Gitterman and Germain's ecological interventions.

The fields of clinical psychology and psychiatry have also undergone changes that at least partially reflected society at large. Freudian psychoanalysis gave way to neo-Freudian and other approaches that were more ego-oriented. The 1950s witnessed the advent of both behavior modification and the Rogerian client-centered approach. These in turn had many variations, including cognitive therapy and many short-term, highly directed types of therapeutic interventions. Today, most helping professions in mental health and social services give considerable credibility to the social support systems approach to treatment. It is not clear whether we have come full circle within these professions and are returning to the roots of social work and mental health and its reliance on natural helpers and community social supports, or whether we are simply following the progress of mental health and social service "science" as we draw on current knowledge of social behavior.

In more recent years, the psychosocial orientation of helping professionals has indicated the recognition that the mind and the physical realm distinguished by Descartes centuries ago are in fact intimately interconnected. But it has been only in the past 10 to 15 years that those in the medical field and scientists in the various related fields of immunology, biochemistry, and the neurosciences have paused long enough to back away from the microscope to see the world.

Some see this return to the knowledge of the unity of mind and body as the third wave of the mental health professions, or as the beginning of a new golden age in the fields of health and mental health. As barriers and prejudices fall between the two camps, new ideas develop and the synergy takes on a force of its own. People can see that when we are embarrassed, we blush; when we are frightened, our pulses rise rapidly. These purely physiological stimuli are no different from other responses, such as the lack of physical stamina or energy when we are depressed or the increase in energy and physical activity when we are happy or in love. We need not be New Age gurus or mystics to see that physical health and mental health are intimately intertwined and that they cannot be examined or understood as separate, disconnected entities. In fact, one cannot be treated without affecting the other.

The development of social support systems is a holistic approach that recognizes that there are multiple causes of human suffering. Our expertise as helping professionals lies in defining the sources of that human suffering and in helping clients develop and strengthen all of the personal resources available to them so that they can get past the suffering and learn and grow from the experience. The "dual worlds" of mind and body, of physical health and mental health, are once again meeting at the philosophical point where new approaches to social systems intervention can be developed. Supporting this progress is research in such developing fields as psychoneuroimmunology, which now shows that the immune system, previously thought to exist independently of the central nervous system, does indeed interact with it.

Professionals in the health sciences are only now recognizing (and some rather reluctantly) that people with positive social support systems withstand the effects of viruses better than others. Although the precise neural pathways are not yet established and may not be for many years, it is increasingly recognized that potentially terminally ill patients with a positive attitude and strong social supports seem to have better recovery rates than others. Research in the suppression of the effects of AIDS, cancer, and other life-threatening diseases is now being seriously pursued by teams of scientists who explore the interconnectedness of mind and body in the causes and the cures of all types of human suffering. AIDS patients in particular may never be "cured" through social support system interventions, but there is little doubt that their conditions will deteriorate if ostracism and social segregation are tolerated.

Finally, for a treatment approach that is evolving as rapidly as the social support system approach, it needs to be recognized that there is much yet to be done. Within the field of social work, the recognition and use of social support were evident with the settlement houses when the profession began. They experienced a resurgence during the 1960s when civil rights and the social aspect took precedence over the psychological in our psychosocial orientation. At present, social workers are developing social support techniques based on a wide and varied body of research but not on a great deal of solid clinical evidence. There have been efforts by social workers and others to empirically validate these strategies (Gottlieb, 1983), but new developments will occur as the future of the field becomes more empirical and research-oriented while concomitantly focusing on social support interventions. If social work continues in the direction of merging research on intervention with social support techniques, the field should witness the development of a variety of highly effective techniques. The future, however, will be in understanding the past, organizing the myriad research findings into some meaningful and coherent set of facts, developing social support interventions based on those facts, and empirically testing and comparing results with rigorous clinical research techniques.

Current Research and Epidemiological Studies

There is a large body of research that attempts to analyze how social support helps. Although there is no clear consensus on precisely what social support is or how it works, researchers and theoreticians alike agree that it serves as a buffer or mediator against the effects of stress (Caplan, 1974; House, 1981). This sort of clear effect can be seen in one longitudinal study that surveyed workers in a factory soon to close about a wide variety of issues related to their job loss (Gore, 1978, 1981). Of particular interest were their perceptions of supportiveness, including how supportive they felt their wives, friends, and other family members were, as measured by the frequency of interaction. Gore found that the negative effects of job loss were significantly less for those who felt they were supported and cared for by others. The support and care provided by loved ones somehow protected these workers from the effects of the stressful loss.

The measurement of such elusive qualities as "happiness" and "satisfaction" have involved social scientists for many years, with Bradburn (1969) initially using a broad survey approach to measure happiness and Cantril (1965) doing the same for satisfaction. These were preceded by early works of Gurin, Veroff, and Feld (1960) in their groundbreaking work for the National Commission on Mental Illness and Health. Their book, entitled *Americans View Their Mental Health,* helped set the stage for the entire community mental health movement by providing an empirical, data-based foundation for it. It substantiated what many psychotherapists and other mental health professionals already knew—that people with socioemotional problems were treated more effectively, efficiently, and humanely if they were allowed to stay in their communities. Caplan (1974; Caplan & Killilea, 1976) at Harvard further supported these findings and described and developed the notion of a support system.

Quantitative analyses, which included the effects of stress, initially centered on the frequently utilized Holmes and Rahe (1967) Schedule of Recent Experiences. This instrument was a useful but rough means of assigning scores or weights to different life events to indicate the level of stress. For instance, the death of a spouse or parent or a divorce are assigned high scores; a jail sentence also is assigned a high score; moving and getting a new job are given lower scores but are nonetheless considered stressful life events. Even though there were attempts to justify the generalization of these constant a priori scores to all people (Holmes & Masuda, 1974), most researchers recognized that the context in which the events occur and individual reactions to them vary considerably (Eckenrode & Gore, 1981). How negatively stressful specific events are to any one individual will obviously be affected by that person's perceptions and feelings. These in turn are a result of the person's own childhood development, earlier life crises (for example, a divorce may be more or less stressful for an individual whose own parents were previously divorced), and biological and genetic makeup. Even a person's ethnic or cultural background has a profound effect not only on how he or she responds to stress, but also on how social workers must gear their interventions to those cultural norms (McGoldrick, Pearce, & Giordano, 1982).

In marriage, there are clear differences between what men and women receive. Most studies indicate that marriage is supportive and positive for men, but less so for women. Single women in general appear to be happier and less prone to being treated in mental health centers or by psychotherapists than single men (Howell, 1981). As a general finding, however, women have more "mental illnesses" than men (Newmann, 1987). This finding is rather consistent whether one collects data from community surveys, first admissions to mental hospitals, psychiatric admissions to general hospitals, outpatient psychiatric treatment, or psychiatrists in private practice. Such epidemiological data must be viewed with some suspicion, however, because prior to 1950, they were collected primarily by using key informants and public records rather than interviews. This method increased the likelihood of finding only "public" disorders (such as antisocial behavior, which is more prevalent among males) rather than private pain or suffering, to which women are socially more sensitive than men. Also, later approaches more carefully assess such symptoms as depression and anxiety, which are more prevalent among women (Howell, 1981, pp. 156–157).

Brenner (1984), of The Johns Hopkins University, examined the social stress effects of economic change primarily during the years 1950 to 1980. He used the following nine indicators of social stress: mortality rates, mortality due to cardiovascular-renal disease, mortality due to cirrhosis of the liver, admissions to mental hospitals, suicide rates, homicide rates, admissions to state prisons, total arrest rates, and rates of major crimes. His economic measures were per capita income (adjusted for inflation), business failures, labor force participation, and unemployment rates. He also took into account and controlled for several external factors, such as smoking, drinking alcohol, and consumption of fat. Table 1-1 shows his results on the effects of economic change for one particular episode—the rise in unemployment in the early 1970s.

Table 1-1. Impact in the United States of a 14.3 Percent Rise in Unemployment during 1973–1974

Psychological Indicator	Change Related to 14.3% Rise in Unemployment (%)	Increase in Incidence of Pathology
Total mortality	2.3	45,936
Cardiovascular mortality	2.8	28,510
Cirrhosis mortality	1.4	430
Suicide	1.0	270
Population in mental hospitals	6.0	8,416
Total arrests	6.0	577,477
Arrests for fraud and embezzlement	4.8	11,552
Assaults reported to police	1.1	7,035
Homicide	1.7	403

Source: Brenner, H. (1984, June 15, Table A, p. v). Testimony before the Joint Economic Committee of Congress. Estimating the effects of economic change on national health and social well-being. Washington, DC: U.S. Government Printing Office.

The chronic diseases, such as cirrhosis and cardiovascular morbidity, as well as total morbidity rates, all have a much longer time lag, so they were estimated to occur within 16 years of the period studied. Although these increases seem small, they are in fact substantial when considered in terms of individual human lives: as shown in Table 1-1, Brenner claimed that nearly 46,000 deaths were attributable to the rise in unemployment alone during the 1973–1974 recession. Brenner (1984) also indicated that the drop in real per capita income in that period accounted for an additional 60,000 deaths. Studies of this sort generally show that economic instability and economic inequity are closely related to and detrimental to the health and social well-being of people, at least on a large scale. These large studies of loosely correlated trends cannot say definitely that factors such as unemployment or loss of per capita income cause increases in suicides or cirrhosis-related deaths, for example, but there seems to be very little doubt that there is a connection.

Questions

1. A list of issues that operationally define aspects of a social support system is suggested. Data could be collected on a handout at initial intake, or by clearly directed questions in the first session or two, or very gradually over the course of treatment as the social worker develops a relationship with the client. Based on your experience and the book's discussion, which of these is the most useful or appropriate?

2. Draw your own social network using the three concentric circles and three sections. Discuss it with a good friend. How and why does yours differ from your friend's? How do age, race, gender, income, marital status, and history of personal/familial moves affect your network?

3. For each of your network members, answer the additional questions suggested for your diagram (for example, Question A: "What is this person's relationship to you?") What are the pros an cons of using both the network diagram and the follow-up questions? Would you use it for your own clients? Why or why not?

4. It is suggested that enduring social support systems based on race and ethnic origin have positive as well as negative results. Based on your personal experience, how do you view homogeneous ethnic or racial neighborhoods from the perspective of social support systems?

5. In your experience and that of family and friends, have you witnessed any indication that healthy behavior, as exemplified by proper exercise, sleep, and diet, has any impact on mental health or attitude? In what ways? Do you see any purpose in discussing or encouraging such physically healthy behaviors for clients who come to you with primarily mental health or social services concerns? Why or why not?

References

American Psychiatric Association. (1987). *Diagnostic and statistical manual of mental disorders* (3rd ed., rev.). Washington, DC: Author.

Biegel, D. E., Farkas, K. J., Abell, N., Goodin, J., & Friendman, B. (1989). *Social support networks: A bibliography, 1983–1987.* Westport, CT: Greenwood.

Biegel, D. E., McCardle, E., & Mendelson, S. (1985). *Social networks and mental health: An annotated bibliography.* Beverly Hills, CA: Sage.

Bott, E. (1971). *Family and social networks* (2nd ed.). London: Tavistock.

Bradburn, N.M. (1969). *The structure of psychological well-being.* Chicago: Aldine.

Brenner, H. (1984, June 15). Testimony before the Joint Economic Committee of Congress. Estimating the effects of economic change on national health and social well-being. Washington, DC: U.S. Government Printing Office.

Burt, R. S., & Minor, M. J. (1983). *Applied network analysis: A methodological introduction.* Beverly Hills, CA: Sage.

Cantril, H. (1965). *The pattern of human concerns.* New Brunswick, NJ: Rutgers University Press.

Caplan, G. (1974). *Support systems and community mental health: Lectures on concept development.* New York: Behavioral Publications.

Caplan, G., & Killilea, M. (Eds.). (1976). *Support systems and mutual help: Multidisciplinary explorations.* New York: Grune & Stratton.

Eckenrode, J., & Gore, S. (1981). Stressful events and social supports: The significance of context. In B. Gottlieb (Ed.), *Social networks and social support.* Beverly Hills, CA: Sage.

Fischer, C. (1982). *To dwell among friends: Personal networks in town and city.* Chicago: University of Chicago Press.

Gore, S. (1978). The effect of social support in moderating the health consequences of unemployment. *Journal of Health and Social Behavior, 19,* 157–165.

Gore, S. (1981). Stress-buffering functions of social support: An appraisal and clarification of research models. In B. S. Dohrenwend & B. P. Dohrenwend (Eds.), *Stressful life events and their contexts.* New York: Wiley.

Gottlieb, B. (1983). *Social support strategies: Guidelines for mental health practice.* Beverly Hills, CA: Sage.

Gurin, G., Veroff, J., & Feld, S. (1960). *Americans view their mental health.* New York: Basic Books.

Holmes, T. H., & Masuda, M. (1974). Life change and illness susceptibility. In B. S. Dohrenwend & B. P. Dohrenwend (Eds.), *Stressful life events: Their nature and effects.* New York: Wiley.

Holmes, T. H., & Rahe, R. H. (1967). The social readjustment rating scale. *Journal of Psychosomatic Research, 11,* 213–218.

House, J. (1981). *Work, stress and social support.* Reading, MA: Addison-Wesley.

Howell, E. (1981). The influence of gender on diagnosis and psychopathology. In E. Howell & M. Bayes (Eds.), *Women and mental health.* New York: Basic Books.

Maguire, L. (1983). *Understanding social networks.* Newbury Park, CA: Sage.

McGoldrick, M., Pearce, J. K., & Giordano, J. (1982). *Ethnicity and family therapy.* New York: Guilford Press.

Newmann, J. P. (1987). Gender differences in vulnerability to depression. *Social Service Review, 61,* 447–468.

Wilson, J. (1987). *The truly disadvantaged.* Chicago: University of Chicago Press.

Chapter 2

Social Support System Intervention: Theory and Practice

Historically, the profession of social work has excelled and led the way in social support system intervention, which is becoming more and more the domain of social workers even as other mental health and social services professionals follow in our path. Rather than being a particular type of treatment such as cognitive therapy or the task-centered approach or a clearly delineated technique such as empathic response or systematic desensitization, social support system intervention constitutes a comprehensive, empirically based framework for social work interventions.

Social work education and the profession itself are steeped in knowledge and values related to the social environment. The profession distinguishes itself from others in viewing all clients in the context of their social systems. Social support can be seen as the basic orientation in social work practice. Even family and group work (Balgopal & Vassil, 1983) by social workers tends to be oriented toward the larger ecological system (Germain & Gitterman, 1980). Despite the grounding of the profession's history and orientation in social support, however, Whittaker and Garbarino (1983) refer to the use of the informal helping system as entering unfamiliar waters for many practitioners. It requires an ecological orientation and an awareness of and ability to deal with the individual in his or her particular situation that are quite different from learning or using a specific technique.

In reviewing this applied use of social support, Whittaker and Garbarino (1983) found general agreement on the following:

1. Social support exists in various forms, such as networks of family and friends, or in created support groups with which professionals link up through formal structures and organizations.

2. There will need to be some fundamental shifts in the roles of professionals if they are to learn to manage the linkages between the formal and informal helping systems.

3. Social support networks or systems serve many purposes and perform many functions that may augment, enhance, or actually constitute the intervention itself in meeting needs ranging from prevention through remediation.

In an article in *Social Welfare Forum*, Maguire and Biegel (1982) described the use of social support networks and "networking" on a continuum of intervention approaches from the microlevel to the macrolevel. They identified the following types of network-based helping relationships: family network interventions, case management, neighborhood helping, workplace support, volunteer linking, mutual help and self-help, and community empowerment. Each of these interventions was also described in terms of the type of helper involved (for example, family, friend, co-worker), the locus of help (such as neighborhood or workplace), the target population, and the type of tie and whether it was natural or created. The last issue to be detailed was the level of help—that is, whether the intervention was considered to be prevention, treatment, or rehabilitation.

This chapter explains and develops as exemplars of social support system interventions the three types of clinical interventions that are the subject of this book: network intervention, case management, and system development. Of these, the primary focus throughout the book is on system development, a highly useful generalist approach that encompasses some of the best aspects of the other two approaches. Before describing these three in more detail, it is necessary to place them in the context of clinical methods used in social work practice.

The Social Support System Model

The social support system model is one intervention approach that social workers can be trained to use. Other examples are psycho-dynamic/ego psychology and behavior modification/cognitive therapy. Each of these types of intervention has its own description and directives, theory, supporting data, and value base (Reid & Epstein, 1972). In somewhat more detail, those four essential elements are as follows:

1. The treatment model—a clear set of directives describing what the intervention is and how to carry it out, what the strategies and techniques involved are, how to assess or diagnose clients, and how best to interact with them

2. The supporting theory—a set of hypotheses that forms the basis and rationale for the approach; deals with the question, Why this approach?; helps put the causes of the problem in perspective so that the ensuing intervention seems logical as a response; and considers the likely effects of the model

3. The empirical base—the data, including case records, published observations, and research from formal studies of the approach, that support the validity of the intervention and/or its supporting theory

4. The value premises—the orientation of the particular approach in terms of three issues: the client's own expressed wishes; the worker's notion of what the client needs; and the protection of the interests of others involved, such as family, friends, and community.

For the sake of comparison, Table 2-1 fills out the four elements in this structure for social support system interventions and also for psychodynamic/ego psychology and behavior modification/cognitive therapy. The section that follows then describes more fully each of the elements for social support system intervention.

Social Support System Interventions: The Model, Theory, Empirical Base, and Values

The Treatment Model. As this approach uses the client's social system for treatment and support, the treatment model for social support system intervention encompasses such techniques as networking extended-family therapy, the use of support groups and self-help groups, stress reduction, and a holistic approach to health and mental health. The model recognizes and uses techniques that minimize the effects of adverse social conditions such as unemployment; difficult marital, family, or job situations; psychological effects of illness and disease; and other stressful stimuli in the environment. The treatment model also works with clients to help them recognize their own part in occasionally making a situation worse by turning such stimuli into

Table 2-1. Essential Elements of Three Diverse Intervention Approaches

Approach	Treatment Model	Supporting Theory	Empirical Base	Value Premises
Psychodynamic/ ego psychology	Uncovering repressed thoughts and feelings, use of transference and blank screen, encouraging insight and understanding of past and of childhood as basis of current problems	Freudian psychoanalytic theory, developmental theory, neo-Freudian theory	Case examples and histories date to early 1900s; outcome research based on projective techniques often cross-validated against each other; case studies describing subjective feelings of relief of problem	Knowledge and expertise of clinician are valued over client's; individual client's problems are paramount.
Behavior modification/ cognitive therapy	Shaping positive and negative reinforcement; treatment of symptoms not underlying causes	Learning theory	Data-based outcome studies of symptom and relief and/or objectively measured behavior change	Client's description of presenting problem is valued over the clinician's; intervention is directed toward symptoms client wants changed or alleviated.
Social support system interventions	Development and use of formal and informal social systems for treatment and support	Systems theory, with some family and organizational theory	Epidemiological and social survey research with network analytical results	Client's tendency to use family, friends, and other natural systems should be encouraged and augmented with professional treatment, coordination, and support.

greater sources of stress than objective evidence and data suggest might be expected—in short, by overreacting.

The Supporting Theory. Social support system theory in general states that people are interconnected in various ways—for example, socially, culturally, politically, racially, and religiously—and that the way they live, act, and feel is affected by these various systems. This "system" is a way of making sense out of the puzzlement or chaos of all of these different patterns of relatedness. Social systems are special orders of systems "composed of persons or groups of persons who interact and mutually influence each other's behavior. Within this order can be included families, organizations, communities, societies and cultures" (Anderson & Carter, 1984, p. 3).

Systems theory has been used in social work as a way of organizing and ultimately applying interventions sensitive to the diverse demands of modern living. Berger and Federico (1985) recommended that social workers use a systems theory perspective and a holistic view in working with clients in order to recognize fully the biological, psychological, social-structural, and cultural sources of behavior. Doing so helps them better understand both obstacles and resources that have a bearing on their clients' problems.

The Empirical Base. The empirical base for social support system interventions involves epidemiologic and social survey systems research as well as varied network analytic techniques that show consistent evidence of a correlation, if not a causal relationship, between the quality and other dimensions of a social support system and mental health (Gottlieb, 1983). This body of research is extremely varied and large (Biegel, Farkas, Abell, Goodin, & Friendman, 1989), but the more frequently cited research projects include the following:

- The longitudinal study by Gore (1978) that followed male industrial workers over several years' time and found that those with close networks of family and friends suffered less depression and fewer somatic disorders than their unattached co-workers.

- The President's Commission on Mental Health, which conducted extensive reviews, beginning with *Americans View Their Mental Health* (Gurin, Veroff, & Feld, 1960) and concluding with the four-volume *Task Panel Report* (President's Commission on Mental Health, 1978); all of these recommended carrying out treatment within the community itself if there is extensive family and community involvement,

142,049 College of St. Francis Library
Joliet, Illinois

instead of using isolation and professional psychotherapy in large inpatient institutions.

- Two separate studies (Pattison, Francisco, Wood, & Crowder, 1975; Tolsdorf, 1976) of schizophrenics and normal individuals, which indicate that the size and certain qualities of the networks of these two groups differ. Schizophrenics have very small but often dense networks composed of family, if they have networks at all. Disturbed but still functional individuals, such as neurotics, have larger but erratically supportive and interconnected network patterns, whereas normal people have the largest and most consistently balanced and supportive interconnected networks.

- Research on treatment outcomes (Maguire, 1979), which indicates that the social support from spouses, family, or even co-workers accounts for more positive outcomes of treatment within community mental health centers than does the type of treatment used, the diagnosis at initial intake, or the amount of time in treatment.

The Value Premises. The value premises of social support system intervention hold that family, friends, and informal sources of support are preferable to any form of therapy that does not extensively involve that informal support system. While valuing and recognizing the therapeutic effectiveness of behavior modification/cognitive therapy and particularly of certain variations of psychosocial approaches and ecological system interventions, this intervention approach places a premium on including the social system as a significant factor in the intervention. The approach encourages and heightens the client's sensitivity to his or her existing social network of family, friends, neighbors, co-workers, clergy, and self-help and support groups. This is done through discussion and through support for the client's participation in and referral to such systems with which the client is already connected. It involves reinforcing potential and existent positive bonds or relationships. In this way, not only is the helping power strengthened, but so is the likelihood of sustaining the positive outcomes that are achieved, because the therapeutic supports become an ongoing part of the client's social system.

Three Major Types of Intervention

As indicated previously, this book and the case examples presented in it focus on three major types of social support system interventions: network intervention, case management, and system development. The reason for the focus on these three uses of social support systems—and particularly on system development—in practice is not that this list is exhaustive or even exclusive. Mental health and social services use literally hundreds of types of interventive approaches, which in turn share numerous techniques, and these three likewise combine much and recognize the need for multiple approaches even with the same client. What the three have in common, however, and the reason for their appropriateness for our purposes, is that they all focus on social support in treatment. All three make extensive use of social support and share the ultimate goal of developing a unified or a coordinated system of help for the client.

Before describing each of the three types of intervention, it is helpful to compare some of their major features. Table 2-2 fills out the four essential elements listed in the preceding section (the treatment model, the supporting theory, the empirical base, and the value premises) for each of the three. As can be seen in the table, network intervention begins with a single identifiable unit and maintains that same unit throughout treatment. Case management, which is not a type of clinical intervention as much as an organizational approach to service delivery for a client with multiple needs, works with many separate, diverse, and often related individuals; coordination is organized through the social worker. And system development is a generalist approach to connecting people with the positive supports they need and turning those supports into a system. It involves locating and organizing diverse individuals, particularly from the client's natural network and through self-help efforts, and unifies them into a connected system centered on the client, often in conjunction with brief treatment.

The primary difference between case management and system development is their reliance on formal and informal resources, respectively. Case managers are social workers who coordinate other professional resources for relatively severe types of dysfunction. System developers are social workers who coordinate the efforts of family, friends, self-help groups, or other informal helpers for less severe disorders or more narrowly focused problems. Network intervention is different from both of them in that it is used only for extremely dysfunctional families in which other psychotherapeutic efforts have essentially failed.

Network intervention as described by its primary developers (Attneave, 1979; Rueveni, 1979; Speck & Attneave, 1973) never attained an extensive following among social work practitioners, prob-

Table 2-2. Social Support System Interventions

Type of Intervention	Category	Treatment Model — Resources	Treatment Model — Process	Supporting Theory	Empirical Base	Value Premises
Network intervention	Clinical intervention	Network of family and friends with some professionals, directed by a team of professionals for a target family	Uniting an extended family/social network, through a series of six orchestrated sessions, into a therapeutic entity	Family therapy plus some systems theory	Very limited, except as generalizations from family therapy results	The family unit and its extended network are valued as the therapeutic resource.
Case management	Organizational administrative intervention	Organization of professional service providers coordinated by a social work manager with secondary reliance on family and friends	Managing multiple separate services to meet a client's diverse psychosocial needs effectively and efficiently	Organizational theory, some systems theory	Business management and administrative research	Multiple diverse resources, each with separate areas of strength, should be coordinated.
System development	System intervention	System of family and friends, organized by a social worker with secondary reliance upon other professionals, and limited, focused treatment	Using informal resources and self-help to develop a system of social supports, augmented with brief treatment	Systems theory plus chosen clinical theories	Epidemiologic research and social survey research related to social support systems vis à vis mental health and stress	Informal resources and self-help efforts, when strengthened, can be used in treatment, rehabilitation, and prevention, often in conjunction with brief treatment.

ably due to its limited application and cumbersomeness for dealing with large numbers of people at the same time. It has not been found effective in clinical studies. Case management is viewed by some as more organizational and administrative than purely clinical (Moxley, 1989; Raiff & Shore, in press). However, system development as described in this book is a highly useful generalist approach that encompasses some of the best aspects of both the other approaches.

The literature and research related to each of the three types of intervention discussed here frequently overlap, and some authors writing on one type include techniques from the other two. Thus, there is overlap both in the literature and in practice. Nevertheless, we will treat the three types as three separate uses of social support for clarification and instructional purposes.

Network Intervention

Network intervention is a clinical approach developed from a family therapy perspective. It uses family, friends, neighbors, co-workers, and other members of the social network of an individual's family. This type of intervention uses a limited number of sessions of several hours duration to orchestrate large numbers of network members through various stages. The first of these is retribalization: the members are told why they are together and are encouraged to get to know one another, sometimes with the help of an "icebreaker" exercise.

In the polarization stage, differing viewpoints are expressed. An example would be the network friends of a drug-abusing adolescent boy indicating that they see the problem as their friend's rejection by his indifferent parents, whereas those in another network faction say that they see the family problem as the boy himself, with his ingratitude toward his well-intentioned parents. Sometimes family network interventions use four to six conveners to move the network members into small subgroups that share common viewpoints.

In the next stage, mobilization, the family's network begins to organize resources to address the problem. For instance, an uncle might offer the drug-abusing boy a part-time job, a teacher might agree to tutor him, and a cousin might offer to introduce the boy to his friends in a church group. After mobilization comes the stage of depression, when the network members realize that the problem, such as drug abuse, is not easily remedied and that much of what had been suggested has already been tried. The possibilities for dealing with the problem are then reconsidered and reworked until the next stage, breakthrough, is reached. At this stage there is a more realistic and enthusiastic commitment to the family and to the family member with the major problem. At the last stage, exhaustion–elation, the family network can end the final session with the knowledge that their support and involvement have been successful.

Case Management

Case management involves the coordination of a variety of professional services and providers to help complement and support each other on behalf of the client without unnecessary duplication of services. It recognizes that many clients of social workers have a variety of psychosocial problems that may require traditional individual treatment, economic help and guidance, child care, assistance with finding a job, education, or any of dozens of other kinds of help. Coordinating such efforts requires a case manager who can assess the needs and organize the providers to deliver their services more effectively. The case manager also works to see that the gaps in services are filled; that providers share their assessments, progress, and methods with each other; and that providers work together to establish a social support system. Social workers are increasingly finding their role to be that of case manager.

Because resources for dealing with social problems continue to diminish as social stresses continue to grow, social workers are called on more and more to manage needed services skillfully so that physical, psychological, financial, and other problems can all be met effectively. Many typical clients of social workers in agencies need medical care from a physician or nurse; counseling from a social worker, psychologist, or psychiatrist; child care from a day-care center; help with finding a job from the state employment office or a vocational counselor; and possibly religious guidance from a priest, minister, or rabbi. Clearly, no individual social worker could provide all of these services. For the most effective help, members from each of the respective professions, or, occasionally, concerned family members or friends, are needed. The case manager must turn these helpers into a coordinated, efficient system to minimize waste of time and money and to avoid duplication of services while maximizing the effectiveness of the individual care providers (Moxley, 1989; Raiff & Shore, in press).

A typical example of a client with multiple needs would be an anxious, unemployed single mother with two young children, one of whom has been hospitalized with pneumonia. Such clients often feel overwhelmed trying to deal with bill collectors, teachers, doctors, and others. If such a client is fairly deficient in extended-family involvement or friendships, it is essential that a social worker manage and coordinate these various professional helpers. It is tremendously beneficial simply to let such a client know that a worker cares, is knowledgeable about the system, and wants to help coordinate needs with available resources.

System Development

System development involves natural social support and self-help efforts. Often conducted in conjunction with other specific treatment interventions, it is a process that complements treatment while establishing a buffer against sources of ongoing environmental stress. Social support development is a generalist approach that can be used with mainstream psychotherapies such as cognitive therapy, behavior modification, or psychodynamic approaches, as well as traditional social work interventions such as the psychosocial approach (Hollis & Woods, 1981) or the ecological approach (Germain & Gitterman, 1980). (Social work approaches are differentiated from others because this profession builds aspects of social support into some of its applications, whereas social support is often completely or largely ignored by the non–social work psychotherapies. In certain ways, social support development, or simply system development, is "built into" the work of Hollis (1964), who so capably combined psychodynamic theory with the social environment, or Germain and Gitterman (1980), who viewed the client's treatment in terms of the ecology and social system in which that person lives. Many social work approaches, such as the problem-solving method or the task-centered approach, are also sensitive to social support even though they share their theoretical bases and applications as much with non–social work brief psychotherapy as with social systems-based social work approaches.)

Self-help efforts can be considered a major aspect of system development. They encompass a wide variety of services, generally from the nonprofessional realm, including organized groups for mutual aid (Silverman, 1978), as well as community grassroots organizations and issue-related political or social action organizations (Powell, 1987). In treatment they are tremendous aids in the development of social support systems. Fellow self-help group members offer, through their empathy, genuineness, and acceptance, the same qualities that social workers are frequently trained to develop in their supportive treatment of clients. Furthermore, when individuals take primary responsibility for their own help, the likelihood of a successful treatment outcome is enhanced because the motivation tends to be strong. The archetypical example, of course, is Alcoholics Anonymous (AA), whose worldwide organization is credited for having done more to treat alcoholics and maintain them in sobriety than any other single professional endeavor could hope to accomplish.

Self-help group members form bonds quickly, based on mutual identification and a shared problem or concern. Their bond is further strengthened through sharing often painful, similar experiences with the group members. Self-help groups are not led by social workers but by other alcoholics (Alcoholics Anonymous), drug abusers (Narcotics Anonymous), relatives of mentally ill persons (Families of Adult Mentally Ill), former psychiatric patients (Recovery, Incorporated), schizophrenics (Schizophrenics Anonymous), parents who have abused their children (Parents Anonymous), or single parents who want and need support and ideas from other single parents (Parents Without Partners). The list, which could go on for pages, includes self-help groups for every major physical disorder and mental health problem.

The animosity that some of these groups had toward professional social workers and others has diminished significantly over the years. Although many of them still are wary of social workers "taking over" their groups, many now welcome the various kinds of support that social workers can provide without undermining the natural group leaders—for example,

- Providing meeting places or conference rooms for meetings
- Sending referrals to the groups
- Consulting with individual leaders about group dynamics or ways to increase membership
- Serving on their boards of directors
- Explaining the group to other professionals who might misunderstand or feel threatened by such groups
- Taking a public position of support for such groups in the setting of community organizations and professional groups in order to increase the self-help group's acceptability and validity
- Notifying the press, with the group members' help and permission, to publicize the existence of the group and the social worker's support
- Providing fiscal support, even if only in the form of use of telephones or coffee pots, secretarial help, or postage and supplies.

A typical example of a client for whom system development should be helpful would be an unemployed, mildly depressed man who is married and has three young children and lives in an area where tens of thousands of blue-collar workers have been laid off. In such situations the level of self-blame, depression, and related family problems grows at an alarming rate. Although individuals such as this man are often fortunate in having fairly stable extended families, or at least church groups, unions, or ethnic groups to help them, more is often needed. Self-help groups specifically developed for the unemployed, where these men and women can discuss the real causes for the layoffs and the ways in which they can realistically respond, are also powerful in their therapeutic effects.

The task of the social worker using system development, then, is to get this man to ventilate and discuss his anger, frustration, and fears, and then to look at what he can and cannot change. The pity and self-blame need to be discussed and recognized as understandable but also as inaccurate and counterproductive. The strength of the resources in this man's extended family should be used by getting him to ask for help from parents, siblings, or neighbors. He could reciprocate by helping them with work or mainly by recognizing that he would do the same for them if their situations were reversed. Having this man draw a diagram of his social network as described in chapter 1 would help him see objectively where possible resources exist among family and friends. His participation in a group for unemployed workers plus a limited number of treatment sessions combine to help him plan and restructure his system efficiently.

The Five Stages of System Development

This section describes the five stages used to develop a social system in practice. It concentrates on system development, the most widely used of the three types of intervention focused on in this book. System development requires a psychosocial educational component in which the clinician sensitizes the client to his or her social situation. In some instances, supports may be virtually nonexistent when treatment begins; in others they may be excessive; and in still others the system may be dormant and need to be encouraged and developed.

System development complements other specific treatment interventions and is typically used in conjunction with them but still follows these five stages: ventilation, assessment, clarification, planning, and restructuring.

Ventilation

The first stage, ventilation, is relatively unstructured. Some clients talk at length about their problems and concerns and even about what they feel needs to be done. Others have little or nothing to say, or what they do say is defensive or avoidant. Many fall between these extremes and begin talking about their problems but then look to the worker for ideas or suggestions about what they should say or even feel.

In this first stage the therapist should encourage the free flow of feelings. He or she will no doubt use nonverbal empathic responses such as nodding, smiling, leaning forward, and otherwise showing concern, compassion, understanding, and encouragement. Verbally, the worker will occasionally be paraphrasing, questioning, and summarizing feelings and issues presented by the client.

The purpose of the ventilation phase is to show clients that they are free to look at feelings and emotions, even seemingly angry or irrational ones. Therapists must be nonjudgmental so that clients will not bias the statement of their feelings in any way. In this open, free-wheeling stage, honest, genuine feelings can be expressed. Not only is this cathartic and freeing for clients, but it also provides the factual basis for the clinician's assessment while establishing a relationship and rapport between clinician and client.

Assessment

Because the second stage, assessment, is for fact gathering, there is more structure and questioning during it than in the first. It is also at this time that the clinician is more clearly shaping the structure of the therapeutic process. Whereas the first stage helps clients relax and unburden themselves as a bond develops between worker and client, the second stage is more directive and begins to lead the way toward the development of a social support system.

This stage, which is particularly important for social support development, is one area where the approaches are not only well developed but are reasonably consistent. Several assessment instruments developed years ago by anthropologists have been adapted to social support practice. Two of those described briefly in chapter 1, involve having the client draw his or her network diagram and then following up this assessment with a series of questions concerning the nature of the support relationship, the frequency of contact, and so forth. This two-part assessment has remained rather consistent for social support interventionists, at least since 1983: Maguire (1983) and Tracy (1990) describe basically the same general approach to assessment.

Clarification

In the third stage, clarification, the social worker seeks a clearer, deeper understanding of the feelings and emotions behind the facts. After the diagramming of the client's network and factual discussion of issues concerning the nature of the relationships diagrammed, the feelings around those relationships must be explored. The second-stage assessment process is difficult for some clients because it forces them to make judgments and distinctions about people who are close to them. But after making those judgments, they need to understand more clearly why, for instance, they see and talk to their mother weekly but rarely see their father. Or why friends from church are seen only rarely when they had once been a close and important source of support. Or what explains their ongoing relationship with a person who alienates other social support system members or who is abusive to them. Clients need to clarify the rationale for relationships. In many instances, the social worker encourages and supports the recognition of the need for strengthening the ties.

In this third stage the client and social worker are engaging in a process of emotionally understanding the advantages and disadvantages of various relationships. The worker helps the client address the often necessary but painful questions relevant to social support system maintenance: Is it really in my best interest? If the client really wants to maintain sobriety, can he or she maintain relationships with alcoholic friends in addition to joining AA? Does the client want to redevelop relationships with extended-family members who were very supportive in the past? What are the pros and cons of moving to a new area or taking a new job? What would it mean to the client personally to make such a move?

In this process of emotionally understanding the facts related to a client's social support system, each component or individual must be considered. For psychodynamically trained social workers, this stage also entails uncovering repressed feelings such as anger or resentment, for example, toward parents or parental figures, which may include spouses. For behaviorists, the focus is more on getting clients to alter behavior to achieve desired outcomes. Cognitive therapists help clients understand how their past negative schema predisposes them to make automatic and frequently counterproductive responses.

Psychosocial therapists encourage an understanding of how the client's feelings and behaviors affect them as well as those around them. Ecologically oriented and other systems-oriented therapists further focus on the ongoing exchanges among their clients' family members, friends, work colleagues, and others as they try to understand and change their condition.

Planning

Planning, which is the fourth stage of system development, involves pulling together facts, data, feelings, and attitudes that have already been explored in relation to the presenting problem by using the social support system in establishing an effective way to proceed.

With many clients this stage follows directly after the detailed assessment in stage two, because once an individual has diagrammed his or her network and examined the various relationships in terms of social support, a logical plan often unfolds quickly. For instance, an alcoholic who diagrams her network may visually recognize two separate clusters of network members—friends with whom she invariably drinks whenever she sees them, and friends at work or her family who do not drink and who have been supportive of her abstinence. The plan for this woman rather quickly becomes one of disengaging from the drinking cluster and spending more of her time with her nondrinking friends and family. To add an element to the social support system that will actively encourage her sobriety, a further step in her plan is for her to attend AA meetings.

A clear plan of action also emerged soon after the assessment for a depressed, isolated, defensive young man who went through what for him was a painful process of trying to come up with names of friends or family. This assessment, which was sensitively done, was followed by a clarification stage in which the young man was encouraged to discuss his loneliness and sense of isolation. He needed help in the clarification of his fears of rejection and with regard to his lack of confidence and self-esteem, which showed up in past social and interpersonal exchanges. The social worker then was able to help him organize a practical plan to rebuild his confidence slowly and carefully.

The social support system that is put together during this stage may include the client joining a support group or reconnecting with one good friend from the past. The plan subsequently builds on these small successes. For example, friends of the client who are involved in structured groups, teams, or organizations are encouraged to help the client get to know others within that system.

There are many advantages to the client joining already existing groups, for example, environmental or political action groups, sports teams, singles clubs, ethnic societies, stamp collectors' groups, or dog or cat owners' clubs, in addition to the more traditional self-help or mutual aid groups with which social workers already engage. Such groups constitute "ready-made" social support systems and tend to encourage social interaction through the sharing of common interests, concerns, or even problems with the client. Basically, however, the plan should be specific to the client's needs, it should build slowly on successive positive attachments, and it should consider connections to a wide variety of clubs, organizations, and groups.

Restructuring

The last stage, restructuring, involves the reorganization of the client's social support system. That involves increasing the quality and quantity of available social supports while possibly decreasing or excising the negative elements of that system.

This stage involves planning, then supporting and encouraging linkages to healthier systems. At times it entails reexamining the fears and histories of problems that had been discussed during the clarification stage. An alcoholic man, for instance, must be helped to connect with the positive influences available to him (family, office friends, and members of AA) while disengaging from alcoholic associates. This is particularly difficult for alcoholics and drug addicts, who often need to be confronted with the fact that their "friends" may care for them only as companions in their separate relationships with alcohol or drugs. A painful but therapeutic point is reached when the social worker confronts the client with stark questions such as, "If your 'friend' had to choose between your relationship and drinking, which would he choose?" or, "If your 'friend' knew that you would die soon if you did not quit drinking, would she support your abstinence?"

Answers to such questions usually point out that, instead of genuine social support systems, alcoholics and drug addicts have separate, lonely companions who relate primarily to their mutual addiction. Friends and even family must be actively engaged to fill this social void. AA or homogeneous alcoholic treatment groups are existing systems that can serve well as transitions to larger social support systems.

Usefulness for Other Approaches

In addition to their use in system development, the five stages can often be observed in the strategies and techniques involved in case management and network intervention. The stages can overlap just as the various techniques of behavior modification, cognitive therapy, and any other treatment approach can. It is necessary, for clarity and for academic purposes, to present any model of intervention as distinct, with its own internal logic, consistency, and strategy, but as experienced social work practitioners well know, interventions on a practical level combine the techniques that work for the individual client.

It should also be pointed out that the five stages constitute not so much a framework for organizing a strategy as the natural, logical progression of steps in system development. The stages are not imposed on the individual; they are simply the normal course of events in social support system development regardless of which particular approach one is using—system development, case management, or network intervention.

These five stages are comparable to those that most social group workers have learned with regard to the development of a group. A group begins with preaffiliation or approach/avoidance, then naturally progresses through issues of power and control, intimacy, differentiation, and, finally, separation. The group worker's task is to help facilitate this natural flow of events. The same is essentially true of the social support system interventionist, who sets the stage by allowing and encouraging a "gripe session" and cathartic discussion of the problem (ventilation), after which strengths and weaknesses of the potential system are looked at (assessment), feelings about that potential system are reconsidered (clarification), a rational approach to the development of the system is worked out (planning), and, finally, changes are made in the system so that it enhances social supports (restructuring).

Within each of these stages, the techniques and strategies that are applied may be borrowed from specific psychotherapeutic models such as cognitive, behavioral, or psychodynamic techniques, and they may also be taken from one of the social support system approaches, that is, system development, case management, or network intervention.

Problems and Limitations

Social support intervention is most appropriate for clients whose primary presenting problems are related to social isolation, whether that is self-inflicted or the result of loss or rejection. The best examples of such clients include reactively depressed individuals such as those dealing with divorce (Chiriboga, Coho, Stein, & Roberts, 1979; Willcox, 1981), or with the loss or feared loss of a job (Clark & Clissold, 1982), money, status, or significant other (Gallagher, Thompson, & Peterson, 1981). Youngsters suffering from a blow to their self-image or from a life crisis are also good candidates (Barrera, 1981), especially because they are so frequently more sensitive to the effects of such traumas than adults are. Many teens and preadolescents, for instance, are acutely aware that their unhappiness comes from having no friends or from being rejected by a clique at school or by a boyfriend or girlfriend.

Others for whom social support intervention is particularly useful are people who are themselves suffering from physical problems (Funch & Mettlin, 1982) or whose loved ones are affected by them. The feeling of loss associated with major physical problems often can be psychologically alleviated through social support. An amputee who shuts himself in his room can more often be helped by another amputee than by someone who has not gone through the same experience. The alcoholic whose isolation and withdrawal into a bottle are rarely affected by traditional one-to-one therapy is often helped by groups such as Alcoholics Anonymous, which exemplifies social support at its best and which can be highly therapeutic with motivated individuals (Henry & Robinson, 1978). The same is true of widows who seemingly gain little from therapy, although the mere presence of another widow just willing to listen or to hold their hand has an immense impact (Silverman, 1980).

Social support intervention cannot be used alone with most major psychopathological disorders as defined in the *Diagnostic and Statistical Manual of Mental Disorders, Third Edition—Revised* (American Psychiatric Association, 1987). Psychotic disorders, major affective disorders, and problems with an organic or chemical etiology will not be sufficiently affected by social support alone. However, social support can be used as a supplement to the primary treatment of such disorders. That treatment, which usually involves both medication and intense psychotherapy, can be significantly enhanced by social support.

Among the problems and limitations associated with social support intervention, the primary one is overreliance on it and unrealistically high expectations for its effectiveness. The early body of research in the 1960s and 1970s that demonstrated its utility was ill-used in the 1980s when social support intervention became a replacement for needed psychotherapeutic interventions. Just as the community health movement fell into disrepute for not being able to improve society, so too will social support interventions, for precisely the same five reasons:

1. *Unrealistic expectations.* Social support interventions alone cannot treat major disorders or community problems. They can augment some other treatments or by themselves they can help isolated people get back into the mainstream of society so they can then function better and improve their own lives. But expecting more than this is doomed to failure.

2. *Insufficient funding.* Social support intervention is not just a cheap replacement for professionals. In fact, if properly used—for example, in some network intervention approaches—it involves orchestrating large numbers of people and well-organized community resources into carefully planned phases of help (Rueveni, 1979). It is more an addition to the therapeutic arsenal than a cheap replacement, and that addition, when properly executed, involves extensive resources from professionals, families, and communities.

3. *Poorly coordinated programs.* The days are gone when professionals could look to government for leadership in coordinating the training, funding, dissemination of information, or developmental research needed to educate the lay public as well as professionals about social support intervention. The federal government seems to play a smaller role in these areas than in past years, and as a result, institutions such as the National Institute of Mental Health are no longer taking active leadership roles, at least in relation to psychosocial approaches.

4. *Insufficient number of trained professionals.* Clinical training of social workers, counselors, psychologists, psychiatrists, and nurses should include courses on social support. At present, universities and large health and mental health programs develop occasional courses in the area, and the fields are gradually shifting more toward this type of approach under the general rubrics of social systems, the ecological approach, network intervention, and self-help and empowerment, but much more training needs to be done much more quickly.

5. *Political climate antagonistic to new programs.* After the Great Society and the subsequent emergence of a more conservative and materialistic climate, the voting public has become

less sensitive to the devastating problems of the socially, psychologically, and economically disadvantaged. Part of this is due to economic forces, and in the face of scarcity, to people's "watching out for themselves." The planned use of social support systems coincided unfortunately with the decline in funding for mental health and social services. Beginning with the Carter administration but rapidly accelerating during the Reagan presidency and continuing with the Bush administration, the social services and mental health professions have witnessed a painful erosion of resources. The beginning of the community mental health movement in the 1960s under John F. Kennedy and the funding of the programs by the Johnson administration did much to bring young social workers, psychologists, counselors, and others into the helping professions even at a time when the intervention methods were primarily in a one-to-one, longer-term mode. Various well-documented studies from that time showed that people with a variety of mental health problems were best served in the community rather than in institutions and inpatient settings. The rationale for this was primarily that family and friends constitute a supportive, therapeutic system that does not necessarily exist within institutions (President's Commission on Mental Health, 1978; Gurin et al., 1960). Although institutions and the professional psychotherapeutic interventions utilized in them can be effective for some, the therapeutic milieu that supposedly existed and that was the basis for the existence of such facilities was actually less therapeutic than what often exists within communities and family structures.

In recent years, social support has been used by many as a cheap replacement for nonexistent professional resources (Schilling, Schenke, & Weatherly, 1988). That is ill-advised, because social support intervention is not meant to be and cannot be such a replacement. Those who have major mental health problems and psychopathological disorders must ethically be treated with the most effective and efficient forms of psychotherapeutic intervention available, whether that is cognitive therapy, behavior modification, or a psychodynamic or Rogerian approach (Hopps, 1986).

Why Social Support Intervention Should Be Used

In most clinical practices, therapists observe that most clients are less abnormal or deviant than they are sensitive and aware. And a common complaint, especially among those who are depressed, is that they feel somehow unconnected to the rest of humanity, that they have no close friends or relatives in whom to confide or who will give them a sense that they are cared for.

This feeling is not just found in people who come in for therapy. For many years, sociologists such as Max Weber blamed this sense of anomie on moving from rural close-knit families to isolated urban living situations, or on industrialization. This same sense of ultimate loneliness, of finally, irrefutably having to live and die alone, is also found in varying degrees in most clients faced with life-threatening, or even role-threatening crises. How do friends and family mitigate these circumstances? Do they in fact offer people protection? If so, how often and how much?

People come in for therapy week after week complaining and worrying that there is something profoundly wrong with them because they feel so alone. They feel that something is missing from their own makeup that all other human beings have. With many such clients, it is sufficient to "problem solve" around objectively and cognitively defined concerns to establish what they can or cannot do to change their situations. In more severe cases, it finally becomes a matter of the client's accepting his or her separateness as an inevitable, yet positive, aspect of the human condition. Once this is understood and accepted, the blame and anger that had been turned inward can end, and these people can accept themseves as "normal," good, and useful human beings without wasting a great deal of psychic energy blaming themselves for their imagined ineptitude and flaws; nor do they need to blame society at large or their own family and friends for insensitivity or lack of caring.

Why should social support intervention be used? Because others not only give us love, support, and guidance, but they also help define us as individuals with separate needs and identities. By actively engaging and interacting with a system of family, friends, and professionals, we each grow and learn about ourselves and our place and purpose in life.

Balancing Support and Separateness

Jacob was a classic example of being unable to get past unresolved anger at one's parents. His parents had gone through a bitter divorce when he was 11, and he was still angry about it at age 22 when I saw him. When he first came to see me he was frightened, hurt, depressed, and angry. During the first few sessions he spewed forth a venomous torrent about his parents, who had apparently put him in the middle of their bitter dispute for about a dozen years.

Jacob had felt torn between his father and mother, but most recently he decided that he hated them both—a feeling that had developed as a result of his profound disappointment soon after graduation from the Ivy League school he had attended on a scholarship. He was having a difficult, stressful time making the transition from being a student and dependent child to being a separate, autonomous adult. Beneath his impressive academic credentials and erstwhile veneer of confidence was an extremely insecure boy, and Jacob became badly shaken when he had difficulty finding and keeping a decent job. His first job after graduation was at a highly competitive stock brokerage firm. It had not been his first choice, but it offered status and good pay. He was fired when the market took a downturn, but Jacob felt that losing his job had more to do with him than with the market.

Within his limited support system, Jacob had developed a pattern of setting people up and then knocking them down because of what he perceived as their "insensitivity" and lack of caring for him. This was particularly true with women; he would date and use a woman sexually, and then completely break off the relationship immediately after sleeping with her. The one exception had been a young woman he had met at college with whom he had a platonic relationship for nearly two years. When a strong relationship developed, she rejected him because he became so critical and negative toward her. This rejection coincided with his job loss. As a result, he moved in with his depressed, needy mother in her small apartment. He spent all of his time alone in his room or berating her for the uncaring and cruel way she treated him.

Jacob tried to use the same pattern with me. At first he vacillated between saying how much he needed me to understand him and give him help and guidance, and how incompetent and uncaring I seemed to him.

During one early session he went on for several minutes about how his parents did not love him enough either when he was a child or now and that it was their insensitivity and continued lack of caring that caused him to lose his job and his only real love. I interrupted him to ask, "So what are you doing about it? You know, the last few times we've gotten together you've told me how unhappy you are with being isolated and dependent on your mother, yet you've done nothing to change the situation. You keep blaming her or your father as if that will help."

"But it's their fault," he yelled.

"Maybe so, but it's your life now. What they did or didn't do years ago or even now is pretty much out of your control. The concern now is what you are going to do, since it's more or less a waste of time talking about or trying to change your parents."

This confrontation was done in a direct but caring manner in conjunction with other aspects of cognitive therapy and social support system development. Jacob already knew cognitively that he had to make changes. We had already discussed his need to develop friendships, and I constantly encouraged him to meet new people, join organizations, exercise, develop linkages to others, and get out of his cramped bedroom. He was also taking an antidepressant that was working extremely well. Jacob was looking for too much from his ungiving parents and, in fact, he was trying to punish them. This was all having relatively little effect on them, but it was draining for him. Gradually he recognized that he slowly needed to redevelop social ties with new friends and to reconnect ties with relatives and older friends, many of whom he had alienated in the past, angry year. I did not disagree that he had a right to be angry at his parents and that at times he should vent the anger. However, his anger over the past had become an end in itself. There was nothing he could do about it but let it out—and then move on with his life.

He did manage to get a decent new job, and there he became friendly with several work colleagues (after first finding them all "boring and stupid"). He also developed a good relationship with a woman with whom he had a great deal in common. Much of our subsequent therapy and counseling revolved around his recognizing his anger over unmet needs, but not displacing all of it. We discussed the fact that his anger was real, and had originated in his family dynamics. However, we also looked at his hostile dependency on his parents and, for a while, on most other potential friends, lovers, or even authority figures. I pointed out that he came across as a needy and hurt person, but also as one who angrily demanded care and affection as a birthright. He came to understand that to get social support, he had to build and develop connections and relationships, and furthermore that such relationships have to be built on give-and-take and mutual caring and trust, not on angry, critical demands that unmet needs be met.

We also discussed the fact that he would need time to rebuild to his old confidence level but that this time his confidence would no doubt be based on a firmer foundation of better understanding. He realized that he would have ups and downs and that occasionally people would not like him no matter what he did. In his recent bout with depression, anxiety, and insecurity, he had both lashed out and clung to his mother, and he needed to recognize that some separateness from her was healthy.

In summary, clients such as Jacob are frequently seen by social workers to help them deal with issues of their own identities separate from their parents. These adolescents or young adults in their early 20s (or sometimes much older people) need to express their fear and anxiety about setting out on their own without parental support. But continuing to focus on the problem for an extended period of time as is occasionally done in psychoanalytic psychotherapy is counterproductive, particularly in the immediate and short term. Whereas young adults frequently have difficulty working through these anxiety-provoking issues related to dependency, separation, and anger, they need to be helped fairly quickly to develop new systems of social support. Helping young adults make a healthy transition from parents to peers for their many personal and social needs is a useful and common social support developmental process.

Helping the Natural Process Work

There is a natural tendency for people to turn to family and friends, if they seek out help at all, when they are feeling depressed or anxious. In a recent research project, nearly half of the 1,211 respondents in a random sample went "nowhere" for help (45 percent), although 18 percent went to relatives, 17 percent to medical doctors, and 12 percent to friends or neighbors. An additional 10 percent went to mental health and social services centers for help with general depression, family arguments, or anxiety (Yamatani, Maguire, Rogers & O'Kennedy, 1989).

The same study (Yamatani et al., 1989) found that this use of natural social supports was generally satisfactory: 61 percent of the respondents were "very satisfied" with the help they received from their relatives, and 90 percent of them were either "very satisfied" or at least "satisfied" with help from friends and neighbors. The study showed that an unusual split develops, however, in relation to satisfaction with the formal versus the informal system. There seems to be a much higher rate of being "very dissatisfied" with the help given in the formal system of medical doctors (almost 27 percent of the respondents were "very dissatisfied") and mental health (29 percent were "very dissatisfied"). These rates contrast with the somewhat lower rates of being "very dissatisfied" with friends and neighbors (10 percent) or with relatives (18 percent).

The authors speculated that the split is primarily because of two factors. First, the formal system of doctors and mental health centers comprises the resource for the most serious, life-threatening types of problems. For instance, an acutely suicidal or psychotic person is taken to a mental health center or to a clinical social worker or physician, not just to a friend or relative. The degree of difficulty and threat to life and happiness are significant in these instances, so the likelihood of a major negative reaction exists when the person is not "cured" or helped appreciably in a short period of time. Thus, the social worker or physician is blamed when a family member commits suicide even if the professional knew the person for only a few hours.

The second explanation that the study suggested for the lower level of dissatisfaction with informal supports is that we are less likely to blame people we know and love than we are to blame a system—even though it includes caring professionals. Parents whose adolescent son just killed himself are more likely to blame the doctor or social worker in the emergency room for perceived incompetence than to blame themselves or one another even though one or both of the parents may have neglected or abused the boy for years.

People's natural loyalty to family and friends who are generally their primary sources of help in any case suggests that professionals should not stand in the way of this form of support for clients but in fact should encourage the natural proclivity of individuals to go to the informal sector for useful and appropriate help. Social support system intervention is little more than the encouragement of this natural flow. Professionals need to recognize that this natural process is also generally the most satisfactory. It works as long as we encourage it, occasionally monitor it, and recognize when the natural social support system is appropriate and when it is more appropriate to channel people into the formal system of social worker, counselor, psychologist, physician, and nurse.

Questions

1. Social support system interventions rely more on social, psychological, and epidemiological research than on clinical interventions. Given this apparent dirth of a solid clinical

research basis, do you view the approach as "solid" in its merit as an intervention? Why or why not?

2. Because the family and social systems are so often the cause of both stress and deviant or maladaptive behavior, how can social workers justify using them for treatment? Are there not inherent risks involved? Discuss these risks and the justification for using the family and social systems in spite of the "risks."

3. There are at least three basic types of social support system interventions described. One of these, system development, is the most general and is used throughout this book as the epitome of social support system interventions. Other than being more encompassing, are there any other differences between it and case management or network intervention?

4. It is stated that social support system intervention is essentially "little more than the encouragement of a natural flow" toward using many and varied available resources. Discuss the evidence supporting this statement.

References

American Psychiatric Association. (1987). *Diagnostic and statistical manual of mental disorders (3rd ed., rev.).* Washington, DC: Author.

Anderson, R. E., & Carter, I. (1984). *Human behavior in the social environment: A social systems approach* (3rd ed.). New York: Aldine De Gruyter.

Attneave, C. (1979). Social networks as the unit of intervention. In P. Guerin (Ed.), *Family therapy.* New York: Human Science Press.

Balgopal, P., & Vassil, T. (1983). *Groups in social work: An ecological perspective.* New York: Macmillan.

Barrera, M. J., Jr. (1981). Social support in the adjustment of pregnant adolescents: Assessment issues. In B. H. Gottlieb (Ed.), *Social networks and social support* (pp. 69–96). Beverly Hills, CA: Sage.

Berger, R. L., & Federico, R. C. (1985). *Human behavior: Helping perspective* (2nd ed.). New York: Longman.

Biegel, D., Farkas, K. J., Abell, J., Goodin, J., & Friendman, B. (1989). *Social support networks: A bibliography 1983–1987.* Westport, CT: Greenwood.

Chiriboga, D. A., Coho, A., Stein, J. A., & Roberts, J. (1979). Divorce, stress and social support: A study in help seeking behavior. *Journal of Divorce, 3*(2), 121–135.

Clark, A. W., & Clissold, M. P. (1982). Correlates of adaptation among unemployed and employed young men. *Psychological Reports, 50(3),* 887–893.

Funch, D. P., & Mettlin, C. (1982). The role of support in relation to recovery from breast surgery. *Social Science and Medicine, 16*(1), 91–98.

Gallagher, D. E., Thompson, L. S., & Peterson, J. A. (1981). Psychosocial factors affecting adaptation to bereavement in the elderly. *International Journal of Aging and Human Development, 14*(2), 79–95.

Germain, C. B., & Gitterman, A. (1980). *The life model of social work practice.* New York: Columbia University Press.

Gore, S. (1978). The effect of social support in moderating the health consequences of unemployment. *Journal of Health and Social Behavior, 19* (June), 157-165.

Gottlieb, B. (1983). *Social support strategies: Guidelines for mental health practice.* Beverly Hills, CA: Sage.

Gurin, G., Veroff, J., & Feld, S. (1960). *Americans view their mental health.* New York: Basic Books.

Henry, S., & Robinson, D. (1978). Understanding Alcoholics Anonymous. *Lancet 1,* 372–375.

Hollis, F. (1964). *Casework: A psychosocial therapy.* New York: Random House.

Hollis, F., & Woods, M.E. (1981). *Casework: A psychosocial therapy* (3rd ed.). New York: Random House.

Hopps, J. G. (1986). Services in a nonexpansionist climate: Some ethical dimensions. *Social Work, 3,* 83–84.

Maguire, L. (1979). *Factors in successful treatment outcome in community mental health.* Ann Arbor: University of Michigan, University Microfilms.

Maguire, L. (1983). *Understanding social networks.* Newbury Park, CA: Sage.

Maguire, L., & Biegel, D. (1982). The use of social networks in social welfare. *Social Welfare Forum, 1981.* New York: Columbia University Press.

Moxley, D. P. (1989). *The practice of case management.* Newbury Park, CA: Sage.

Pattison, E. M., Francisco, D., Wood, F. H., & Crowder, J. A. (1975). Psychosocial kinship model for family therapy. *American Journal of Psychiatry, 132,* 1246–1251.

Powell, T. (1987). *Self-help organizations and professional practice.* Silver Spring, MD: National Association of Social Workers.

President's Commission on Mental Health. (1978). *Report on the task panel on the nature and scope of the problems.* Washington, DC: U.S. Government Printing Office.

Raiff, N. R., & Shore, B. (in press). *Advanced case management.* Newbury Park, CA: Sage.

Reid, R., & Epstein, L. (1972). *The task-centered approach.* New York: Columbia University Press.

Rueveni, U. (1979). *Networking families in crisis: Intervention strategies with families and social networks.* New York: Human Science Press.

Schilling, F. J., Schenke, S. P., & Weatherly, R. A. (1988). Service trends in a conservative era: Social workers rediscover the past. *Social Work, 33,* 5–9.

Silverman, P. (1978). *Mutual help groups.* Washington, DC: U.S. Government Printing Office.

Silverman P. (1980). *Mutual help groups: Organization and development.* Beverly Hills, CA: Sage.

Speck, R. V., & Attneave, C. (1973). *Family networks.* New York: Vintage.

Tolsdorf, C. C. (1976). Social networks, support and coping: An exploratory study. *Family Process, 5*(4), 407–417.

Tracy, E. M. (1990). Identifying social support resources of at-risk families. *Social Work, 35*(3), 252–258.

Whittaker, J. K., & Garbarino, J., and Associates. (1983). *Social support networks: Informal helping in the human services.* New York: Aldine.

Wilcox, B. L. (1981). Social support in adjusting to marital disruption: A network analysis. In B. H. Gottlieb (Ed.), *Social networks and social support.* Beverly Hills, CA: Sage.

Yamatani, H., Maguire, L., Rogers, R., and O'Kennedy, M. L. (1989). *The impact of social/economic change on households among six communities in western Pennsylvania.* Pittsburgh: University of Pittsburgh School of Social Work.

Chapter 3

Working with Depressed Individuals

This chapter first examines some major problems and issues that a social worker is likely to encounter in helping clients develop social support systems. It then focuses on a large client population—depressed people—that not only is seen frequently by social workers but that also is particularly amenable to social support interventions and for whom the problems in using social support come up regularly in treatment.

Problems in Using Social Support

This section discusses five major problems related to the use of social support for individual clients. Although not meant to be all-inclusive, this list does offer the social worker an idea of the range of practical issues to be considered in working with individuals. The five problems, each described in a subsection below, are as follows:

1. *Faulty perceptions of reality*—individuals' often incorrect perception of the actual or potential strength of their social support systems.

2. *Parataxic distortion and poor self-esteem*—the negative and inaccurate way that clients often feel about themselves and their "worth," causing them to misinterpret help and support even when they do receive it.

3. *Depression*—a name for a constellation of behaviors and attitudes (such as lack of energy, self-hate, a sense of futility, and alienation) that frequently work against the development of a social support system.

4. *Individuality of need*—the specific nature of different types of problems that require different types of social support. The varied problems further require that social workers carefully design approaches to meet the specific social support needs, whether for guidance, referrals, listening skills, treatment, money, jobs, or a home. Defining the specific type of needed social support with the client is a skill that is not yet developed sufficiently by most social workers.

5. *Deficient social skills*—the faulty ability or complete inability of many clients to develop relationships appropriately and effectively with others.

Faulty Perceptions of Reality

One important practical aspect of developing social support for clients relates to the accuracy of their perceptions of reality regarding social support. It is not uncommon for social workers to interview people who feel alone and uncared for in the midst of large, supportive families, or for a client to claim to have many friends when the worker knows he or she has none.

Research has shown that clients' perceptions of their social support and the reality of that social support for them as individuals may be quite different. Lakey and Heller (1988) found no significant relationship between the two. Applying this to counseling situations, social workers need to learn to help clients be more sensitive to the difference between what they realistically have and what they do not have as supports in their environment. They can also help clients recognize the positive social supports already available to them. This realization in turn translates into a change of both attitude and behavior toward their sources of social support.

Some may say that clients' perception of the support they have or do not have constitutes their own reality and that if they feel they have enough support, this is not an issue. However, social workers rarely see clients who are alone and happy with being alone. Those who really are content with that situation should indeed be left alone, but clients who for some reason are dissatisfied with themselves, their lives, marriages, jobs, or friends want and need help. All of these kinds of dissatisfaction can relate to problems in the social support system.

Perceived lack of social support is often a function of unrealistic expectations. A hostile, dependent young man whose problems originated in an enmeshed relationship with his mother that has continued since infancy will expect others to love him and identify with him—almost fuse with him—to feel his pain and somehow to take care of that pain. With such expectations, which can never be fulfilled in any healthy relationship, the client becomes angry at others who invariably fail to give him what he wants. To him, his social support system is deficient or even uncaring, when in fact his mother and others may have tried ceaselessly to help him and to be there for him. His perceptions will be that they did not care enough; the reality is that they tried too much, but ultimately could never meet his expectations and were therefore angrily dismissed as being uncaring and unsupportive.

Parataxic Distortion and Poor Self-esteem

Another problematic category of clients is those with low self-esteem. Not only do they see themselves as unlovable, but they act on that belief. Thus, even when others try to be supportive, their behavior is frequently misinterpreted. That is, positive attempts at connecting with another are misinterpreted by the person with low self-esteem as being negative or critical, which turns the interaction into a negative message based on a negative self-image rather than the intended positive social support message. This process, which is called parataxic distortion, involves a self-fulfilling prophecy. For instance, a 30-year-old woman with low self-esteem who is a single mother and whose life consists of a demanding job and three even more demanding children may begin to see herself as an unlikely person to befriend. Attempts by well-meaning neighbors to help watch the children may be angrily rebuffed because she interprets them simply as a way to keep her overactive children quiet. She may similarly rebuff many who ask her out, interpreting the invitations as pity rather than the genuine interest that it may be. Instead of accepting and benefiting from the social support offered, she will misinterpret the offers as attempts to control her children and as pity, thus reinforcing her perception that she is a poor mother and a pitiable human being. Parataxic distortion with low self-esteem is also a common problem in groups (Yalom, 1985), because it distorts communication and interactions.

Another way of looking at this same phenomenon comes from the fact that it is more logically consistent for individuals with low self-esteem to seek help (Nadler, 1986), feeling they are generally inadequate to accomplish needed tasks on their own. Fischer, Godd, Nadler, and Chinsky (1988) found that individuals with low self-esteem are more likely to seek psychiatric treatment than are people with high self-esteem, but how they interpret the help may be a problem.

Depression

Another large client population that misinterprets social support is depressed individuals. For them this is such a pervasive problem and so appropriate for social support system intervention that the next section of this chapter is devoted to it. Following are a few brief comments on the subject. Some depressed clients do use social support extensively, so social workers need to be careful in assessing whether the particular depressive symptoms of a client work for or against this approach. Depressed people often categorize their social systems with simple good-or-bad, black-or-white labels (Wright & Beck, 1983). Unfortunately, the vast preponderance of their social stimuli eventually ends up in the "bad" category. Depressed men and women see helping attempts by family and friends as negative or hostile rather than as constructive. The brother who calls or drops in, for example, seems nosy, or demanding; the neighbor who brings food over is perceived as subtly criticizing the depressed person's ability to cook and capacity to take care of himself or herself. The results are similar for both depressed clients and those with low self-esteem: potential social support is misinterpreted and rejected.

Individuality of Need

Another factor related to the discrepancies between perceived and actual sources of social support involves more precise operational definitions of social support. The goal of the social worker is never merely to provide a social support system for a client. The goal is to help the client work through some type of problem. Social support systems are only the means to an end. Therefore, they must be carefully tailored to the specific requirements of the individual client and his or her present need. Social support might consist of giving advice, listening, or offering a variety of psychosocial resources or even money or jobs. It also involves significant factors that are difficult to quantify or to define clearly, such as caring, affection, or even love, and the closely related issue of how they are expressed. The fact that someone is loved is irrelevant in terms of social support if the love is expressed sullenly or abusively.

Because the types of social support offered and the ways in which they are given must be geared to the client's specific needs, it is not enough just to encourage a person to develop friendships or to reconnect with his or her family. If a person has low self-esteem, obtaining the type of social support needed will entail a low-risk process such as joining an existing, welcoming group of people with similar issues. Depressed people need a more assertive intervention that will help them find activities or people who quickly tap in to any positive feelings that they have. Depressed people often need to be guided through the process of finding others who understand their condition, such as other widows, or people who have recently become unemployed or divorced.

Some clients need other people just to listen to them; others need a job or money. In other words, meeting the needs, overcoming the particular barriers, and finding or utilizing the available resources must all be accomplished in terms of the individual social support needs of the client.

Deficient Social Skills

Another problem frequently encountered in using social support systems in practice involves the client's ineptitude or lack of social skills. Some clients do not know how to develop relationships or to connect meaningfully with others. This may be because of poor parental modeling, a deprived social environment, or various psychological or behavioral deficits. By adulthood the capacity to develop such skills may be limited for some, but in any case the development of skills must begin with the client's ability. The social worker may even need to instruct the client to greet people or to say hello to specific individuals.

Because many of these clients have never dated or been close to others even though the desire to do so and the potential may exist, they must often be cautioned to take things slowly and to remember that developing supportive relationships takes time and effort. Their expectations need to be openly discussed and analyzed in terms of their likelihood of success. For instance, a withdrawn, obese, middle-aged man who expects an attractive bank teller half his age to date him may be in for disappointment. At the least, he needs to discuss or even role play ways to meet people, to engage them comfortably in conversation, to find common interests and backgrounds, and to know when and how to become more intimate with another. These skills, which most people take for granted, are not only lacking in many clients of social workers but are even frightening. The fear of failure, rejection, or being made to look foolish are all intimidating and frequently stop clients from even trying to establish relationships. A slow, careful, gradually escalating approach to social support development that concentrates on social skills education may be difficult, but rewarding.

Emotionally, individuals with deficient social skills need the opportunity to discuss, probably for the first time, their genuine, unguarded fears and hopes in relation to support from others. What do they fear and why? Even if their life history tells them that people can be manipulative and abusive, can they see the possibility of a supportive and caring relationship? Can they trust and let their guard down in hopes of having someone enter their lives long enough to support them through a crisis, or for a longer time?

Sometimes the answer to these questions is no. Certain individuals—for example, many with antisocial and schizoid personality disorders, as well as psychopaths—seem not to be able to participate in a social support system. Also, extremely narcissistic people and those with significant organic impairment may benefit outwardly from involvement in a social support system, but their capacity to reciprocate may be so limited that the system cannot be maintained without continued professional support. In those relatively rare instances where the capacity to engage meaningfully and reciprocally in a caring relationship is missing, the social skills education approach is fairly limited, at least in terms of therapeutic gains.

If there is to be positive, constructive benefit from social support, the support must be recognized and accepted by the client, a process that is important but often difficult. Its difficulty can be seen, for instance, in an individual who, having grown up enmeshed with his needy mother, is understandably frightened of any close relationship for fear of being engulfed and losing his own autonomy. Or in a woman who, seeing herself as unworthy of affection, views the offer of help as either manipulative or pitying. Or in the depressed client who prefers isolation to the demands of interacting with others.

Others have also addressed the many different types of problems related to actually receiving social support. In a clear, well-organized table entitled "Individual-Based Barriers to Social Support: Attitudinal and Behavioral Correlates," Pearson (1990, p. 78) lists three barriers to social support: withdrawal, ineptness, and alienation. The related "attitudes" for withdrawal include low self-esteem, fear of criticism, and the expectation that other people will not be of help. The behaviors associated with the withdrawal barrier include avoiding others, self-depreciation, quietness, aloofness, low self-assertion, and not asking for help. The second barrier, ineptness, is related to an attitude of ambivalence toward others, with the associated behavior of being mildly inappropriate. The third barrier, alienation, is related to self-centeredness, suspicion, and insensitivity, with the associated behaviors of being annoying, demanding, manipulative, nonreciprocative, exploitative, and aggressive.

These barriers, attitudes, and their related behaviors must be assessed and analyzed with regard to each individual client. Objectively, network issues such as the number of people available, the types of support offered (listening, jobs, advice, and so forth), the frequency of interaction, and the density of the network (that is, how close and cohesive the network is, defined as the number of people who know each other) must be assessed. For social support intervention to work, the appropriate type of acceptable and available help must be effectively and efficiently offered to the client so that it will actually be used.

In an excellent review of the social psychological influences on help seeking and support, Fischer et al. (1988) caution against indiscriminate use of the social system for clients. There may be conflict between the system and the client, or the client may become overly reliant and eventually alienated if the system fails him or her, and many peer resources have not been adequately researched to find out how truly helpful they are. The authors suggest that, based on their review of the research, practitioners should first of all be cautious in using outside resources for clients whose networks might not tolerate it, although if other network members have already used a particular outside resource it might be suggested. Second, practitioners should consider clients' ability to communicate their needs effectively with their networks. As can be seen, there are a variety of problems and barriers related to help seeking from individuals, particularly depressed and resistant clients. The following is an example of such a client.

Treating Depressed Individuals

The Motorcycle Man

John was a 45-year-old factory worker whose second marriage was in jeopardy after its first four years. John was angry at his wife, hated his job, fought with his neighbors, and had no friends or even

*relatives whom he could tolerate or who would talk to him. His only
sources of pleasure were riding a motorcycle and working on a train
set that he had in his basement. When he came in for treatment, even
these two activities had been abandoned for months because they were
"stupid" or a "waste of time and money." He was referred to me by
his employer, who pressured him into entering treatment. John's
attitude toward me was overtly antagonistic, and initial attempts at
examining even modestly positive options were met with ridicule.*

*Based on John's interests and history, I initiated some discussion
of his past social supports. He said he used to ride his motorcycle
with a group of friends until about two years earlier. A discussion of
where these people were and how he might reach them quickly led him
to declare that they were all jerks anyway and that I must not be much
of a social worker if I wanted him to hang around with a bunch of
drug-abusing criminals. I made it clear that this was not my intent but
that it might be advisable for him to consider some small contacts with
at least one person who had once been a friend. He agreed to this but
reported back the following week that this person—whom he had
called once during working hours—had not been home. We discussed
the rationale for developing friendships and being engaged in social
activities and the contradictions between his avowed interest in such
activities and his lack of concerted effort to connect. We again
discussed how and why he should call this former friend and other
people he knew. We also agreed that he would bring his wife to the
next session, which was the fourth. He had also been put on
antidepressant medication, which was clearly beginning to affect him.*

*John's wife was an outgoing, attractive, articulate woman. Not
only did he smile for the first time during the sessions, but he seemed
to change considerably in her presence. He was very proud of her but
was also intimidated by her forceful personality and verbal and social
skills. In the three subsequent sessions, we all discussed how she
could listen more and advise less, and slowly and comfortably help
John become more relaxed with others.*

*By the 12th and final session, John had not only begun
motorcycling with one old friend, but he and his wife, at her initiation,
had actively become involved with two other couples. John also
redeveloped his relationship with his 12-year-old son from his
previous marriage. After some initial problems and anger from his
son, who had felt abandoned, John managed to see the boy weekly. I
worked closely with him as he processed the angry reactions of his son
and his own feelings of guilt and hurt. He had repressed his great
desire to see his son out of fear of dealing with the boy's*

understandable anger. Once past that stage, the relationship developed well.

John's depression diminished as he gradually learned to give and take in relationships with others. His wife and son both needed him just as much as he needed them, but there had been a series of crises a couple of years before treatment, and depression had developed. He had needed a way to break out of his depressed isolation. This intervention involved a slow, gradual building of a social support system.

As described in the preceding case example, system development for this client was fairly typical and followed the five stages discussed in chapter 2. Ventilation involved the first few sessions, during which John complained about being pressured to come in but even more about his general unhappiness, despair, anger, and sense of hopelessness. As a traditional working-class male, he was reluctant to talk about feelings and emotions but was able to do so with considerable encouragement and support.

In working with relatively closed, depressed, and defensive clients, the ventilation period is particularly helpful in letting out a great deal of repressed emotion as well as in forming the basis for a new type of relationship. Some depressed clients have difficulty expressing their true feelings, and many have kept them in for years, thus exacerbating their depression or feelings of being alone or deviant. The ventilation stage allows the person to let these feelings out so that they can be explored and dealt with realistically.

The assessment focused on actual and potential social supports. Therefore, completion of the network diagram and discussions of family and friends followed. John's depression was so severe that he was negative about virtually everyone in his system. Several members of his support system were indeed not helpful or constructive, so they were discounted as individuals with whom he might possibly reconnect as friends.

This assessment phase for depressed clients can be very therapeutic in itself, although it should not be attempted too early, because the pervasive negativism of such clients distorts their perceptions. Typically, they initially say they are "being realistic" by assessing virtually everyone and everything in their lives as uncaring, insensitive, or just plain bad. They see social support systems as being nonexistent. The social worker needs to sensitize the client carefully to the real existence of at least some potential supports, while pointing out that the client's perception is not realistic but very unrealistic and negatively biased.

The clarification stage consisted of a more detailed examination of John's relationships with friends from his motorcycling days as well as with neighbors and co-workers whom he had alienated or from whom he had distanced himself. Discussing his wife, his marriage, and his son from his previous marriage was also part of this stage. I encouraged him to talk about what he was receiving and giving in each of these relationships. Furthermore, for the first time in his life he was not only encouraged, but required, to be absolutely honest in clarifying the pros and cons of each of his closest relationships. He had complained about his wife, but confronted with the option of increasing or decreasing his ties with her, he quickly chose to commit himself more to the marriage.

Planning involved bringing John's wife into the sessions as well as developing a strategy for reinvolving him with life. He had avoided his wife for a couple of years, but in their joint sessions it became clear that he was very dependent on her in a positive way—that is, he relied on her to help him interact with others. She welcomed the chance to be involved. In fact, the sessions included three-way discussions of how she could help and support her husband without taking over and undermining his less-developed social skills. She helped devise a plan for having other couples over and for encouraging John to go out occasionally with one other motorcycle enthusiast. She also let him know that she wanted him to reconnect with his son from his previous marriage.

For other clients during the planning stage, reinvolvement often involves groups—for example, self-help groups, church, singles organizations, or sporting activities. It is often easier, more efficient, more effective, and less threatening for depressed clients to link up with existing groups or organizations in which, at the outset, relationships are less threatening and more structured. The possibilities are endless, but the client must come up with suggestions. These plans must take into consideration not only the degree of depression (severely depressed individuals cannot even engage well in this process, let alone in the next stage), but also the social skills, comfort, background, and interests of the individual.

The restructuring stage for John involved changing his activities to include doing things with other couples, his son, neighbors, and a few friends from work. John needed help in rearranging his time so that it included interaction with those who cared about him. He needed to break the depressive isolation that he had built around himself. He gradually became actively involved with his son's baseball team, and together they even joined a father-son club to share their old mutual interest of electric trains.

Depressed people often describe themselves as feeling alone, unloved, unworthy of love, and incapable of giving love. Their symptoms usually include lack of energy and motivation, inability to develop or even maintain social ties, sleeping and eating disorders, and general lack of interest in life with a frequent, overwhelming feeling of hopelessness. Suicidal risk is heightened, and the overt act of cutting out social supports (perhaps telling friends and relatives to leave them alone) diagnostically indicates a likely suicide attempt soon thereafter.

Depression is a lonely disorder. It makes people question their self-worth and the affection of others. It affects self-esteem and confidence and feeds into people's lifelong doubts about their real worth and reason for existing. In the case of impulsive adults or adolescents who are depressed, a crisis, and particularly some form of major loss, often precipitates a suicide attempt, which is the ultimate expression of feelings of lack of self-worth.

Many depressed clients, particularly those with rigid personalities, develop a tendency to see the world as black or white, good or bad. When life is viewed this way, anything short of perfection is failure, and virtually all relationships in some way seem fatally flawed. As a result, depressed people develop a very narrow perspective (Burns, 1978), eventually coming to see themselves and their social environment as horribly deprived or mean. They perceive those around them as not really caring, or as being downright hostile. Their polarized view of life becomes increasingly negative as they convince themselves that no one cares, or that even if somebody does care, they could never change their own hopeless lives enough to really enjoy life. Their own actions turn into self-fulfilling prophecies: they describe how they did try to call a friend but that friend never returned their calls, or they explain that they tried to talk to someone last week but that person was too busy to be bothered with them.

To the very depressed, reality is negative. Attempts by friends, relatives, or well-intentioned but poorly trained clinicians at cheering them up or logically dissuading them from their viewpoint may have the effect of further convincing them that they are right and that friends, relatives, and even professionals are very unrealistic and insensitive to the real pain suffered by the individual or just cold and unfeeling. Such attempts are therefore seen as further evidence that those support system members are of no help.

The treatment of depressed individuals involves the gradual creation of a social support system; a cognitive, reality-based assessment of the causes and "cures" of the depression; and a variety of other psychosocial or even psychopharmacological aids. Depressed clients need to be given support while being gradually encouraged to do things for themselves. They need to be sensitively confronted with the fact that their current feelings are extreme, and that reality is more moderate. While logical debate or attempts at persuasion are often counterproductive, the accurate clarification of facts, cognitions, and perceptions tends to work well (Wright & Beck, 1983).

In the cognitive model of depression, the client is seen as using a selective negative bias in viewing experiences. This negative bias is based on earlier, primitive schemas. Certain automatic thoughts take over, and they are characterized by illogical reasoning because of those schemas. As these negative appraisals of the person's situation persist, his or her mood becomes sad, and other symptoms such as loss of motivation, inertia, thoughts of suicide, or general malaise and lack of interest all worsen. Positive, more balanced perspectives are ignored or seen as relatively insignificant in comparison with what the depressed person sees as overwhelming evidence of his or her worthlessness, or hopelessness, or as the impossibility of anything good or constructive developing (Wright & Beck, 1983).

As stated, directly attacking this belief system has little positive effect and is often counterproductive. The treatment must therefore orient itself instead toward a collaborative process in which the social worker works realistically with the client to increase rationality in thought and to devise strategies such as developing social support systems and increasing the quality and quantity of activities and of social ties to potentially helpful people. Homework assignments are given often and are discussed regularly to support and monitor the client's progress.

The social worker may also focus in on inaccurate assumptions made by a client and on his or her automatic thoughts—for example, someone did not say hello so they must hate me. The social worker spends time questioning the client's database and perceptions of reality and may encourage the person to examine alternative hypothesess—for example, maybe the person that they said hello to did not hear them. Such alternative explanations should be elicited from the client rather than presented by the social worker.

It is also critical to examine the negatively distorted perceptions of the support system. Depressed clients might initially indicate that they have no friends or reliable family members, because that is consistent with their negative schema. The social worker therefore needs to gradually work with clients in realistically and cognitively examining their network (which may well be very small and nonsupportive) with a viewpoint toward gradually building it up. Support system development must involve an assessment, but because that initial assessment is probably unrealistically negative, the worker will need to focus on weak linkages from the past or present as starting points. Depressed clients need to learn that social systems are built gradually over time and with effort. Depressive black-or-white, all-or-nothing thought processes inhibit such slow and gradual developments. Therefore, clients frequently need to be reminded that their support system will not be developed overnight and that it *will* grow with effort and planning but not as a result of some intrinsic personal quality such as being lovable or being "good people."

The social worker must be cautioned not to try to cheer the client on or in any way minimize the fact that it takes not only work but a fair degree of personal risk taking to try to build such supports. The client will invariably become discouraged, and when quick gratification does not develop in the form of a good and caring friend or a loving relationship, he or she will tend to revert to the automatic thought of being worthless. At that point the worker must again ask the client precisely what facts support that perception.

Fortunately, success breeds success, and small steps in the development of social support lead to bigger steps at an accelerating pace. One 10-minute phone call to an old high school friend may well be the first step back up the ladder to self-esteem and diminished depression. If a person can call one old friend, he or she can also try to join or at least observe one self-help group activity, go to a church outing, take part in a choir practice, or watch a nephew play basketball.

These small steps are to be supported but never overly praised by the social worker. To do so would be to fall into the very pattern that one is attempting to change for the client, that is, of perceiving reality in extremes of good or bad, won or lost. The reality is that a small social step is a small social step in the direction of a gradual development of a social support system. The client frequently needs to be taught or perhaps just needs to relearn social skills.

Friendships are developed by showing and expressing concern about others. Friendships are put at risk when one becomes overly dependent, demanding, or critical of real or perceived "flaws" or slights. Thus, the client sometimes needs to discuss his or her tendency to be overly critical of others who fall short of perfectionistic standards. He or she may need to appraise past interactions realistically to see that unrealistic criticism has resulted in distancing a relative or friend.

This is a learning process in two ways. First, it helps the client master social interpersonal skills that may be deficient. He or she really must learn how to develop and slowly nurture friendships. Second, the process helps the client examine himself or herself in a nonjudgmental, realistic, and balanced way. Thus, if someone turns down the client's invitation to go to a movie or out on a date, the client must be helped to realize that there are many possible reasons for this other than extremely negative ones such as the automatic thought that the other person hates them or thinks they are completely worthless. More realistic possibilities include previous engagements or a desire to go more slowly with the development of a relationship. Being turned down is not a defeat, nor is acceptance a "win." Interpersonal interactions and the gradual development of a social support system all have to be put into a realistic cognitive framework and viewed as a gradual process of building a system of support.

The Reversible Couple

Sally was a 38-year-old saleswoman who had spent the early years of her marriage on the road making an adequate living. She had quit that hectic, lonely life six years earlier to spend more time with Bob, her 30-year-old husband, a very cold but successful computer systems analyst. They had a nine-year-old daughter with whom each had an excellent relationship.

Sally was depressed because Bob had admitted to having a series of affairs, mostly one-night stands, although a couple of them had gone on longer. After multiple sessions, she also told the social worker that she had "rescued" her husband when he was 19 from a life of drug addiction. What she did not say for a long time was that she had also been involved in affairs in the first few years of their marriage and had stopped only when her husband had become suspicious and threatened to leave her several years earlier.

She had begun having affairs while she was a traveling saleswoman. He began his only after she quit her decent-paying job on the road for a lower-paying one near him. In the meantime, he had earned his bachelor's degree and had focused his considerable energy, intelligence, and drive on his career.

When the social worker began seeing her, Sally was earning $15,000 a year selling magazines by phone, and her husband had just been promoted to a $40,000 job as director of personnel at a new computer company. His new boss was a vice president with whom he had had an on-again, off-again affair that Sally knew about. She could not, however, get him to stop or even to discuss the matter other than his saying, "You're in no position to lecture me." Their own marriage was cold and hostile; Sally felt that he was in control. She was severely depressed, suicidal, and feeling unloved.

"I know I deserve it, but damn it, I can't take this anymore. Last night he came in again at 3 A.M. and got sick in the bathroom. I asked him where he'd been, and he just said to leave him alone. I know he's with some other woman. I sometimes wish I could leave him, but I love him. He's everything I ever wanted," she would say.

Sally had become passively but hostilely dependent on her husband over the past few years. As his career had progressed, hers had gone downhill. Their marriage had also paralleled that pattern: initially she had had all of the power in the relationship and he had been passively dependent on her. Now he had the money and the job—and the affairs.

Sally's goal was to "save" the marriage by getting her husband back. She often cried in the sessions as she discussed her love for him and her anger at feeling rejected by him for other women, or at least a couple of women she knew of. She had become unable to respond sexually on the few occasions he was willing to sleep with her, and she saw this as a possible additional reason for his lack of interest and disdain.

Because he was adamantly unwilling to come in for joint sessions and she was increasingly dependent and "clinging," yet overtly angry at him, the social worker encouraged her at least to stop pursuing him. Their relationship had deteriorated to such a state that the more pitifully she pursued him the more savagely he ridiculed her and pursued other women.

The social worker worked with Sally in an effort to develop her self-esteem outside of her marriage. She also pointed out several patterns that Sally had developed, including the most obvious one of actually increasing her husband's disdain for her by desperately clinging to him. It was clear that the more Sally pursued Bob in this depressed, needy way, the more repulsed he was by her. As hard as it was for Sally, the worker encouraged her to put herself in his place. Because that had been the situation during the years when Sally was having affairs, it was painful but eye-opening for her to realize that in part he was getting revenge. But she also realized that she too would be repulsed by a clinging, desperate, and depressed spouse.

System development in this case had to begin with detachment and with developing a sense of self-worth. Sally's diminished self-esteem had made her desperate pursuit of her husband counterproductive even in terms of reconciliation let alone in terms of her own self-worth. After letting her talk out all of her anger and frustration, the social worker had Sally examine the harsh reality of the futility of her behavior. Although the worker had major doubts about the ultimate feasibility of salvaging this marriage, she was careful not to question that initially, because the idea was too frightening for Sally in her suicidal and depressed state. However, they focused instead on separate areas in her life where she did get satisfaction and some sense of being needed for herself. That sense of self-worth was almost totally met through her daughter. In fact, her recurring discussions of suicide were forestalled only by discussing how much her daughter loved and needed her.

As the depression and suicidal tendencies abated after the stages of ventilation, assessment, clarification, and gradual cognitive problem solving, a sense of anger developed. Gradually but erratically Sally became more successful in her job, while at the same time becoming more confident and angrier at her husband for his rejection of both her and her daughter. The social worker strongly reinforced her redevelopment of her relationship with her parents, who turned out to be extremely supportive. She began opening up (sometimes inappropriately) to others both at work and in a slowly developing social life. She almost lost her job at one point when she was beginning her upward phase out of the depths of depression and suicide but through the angry phase. Because of this, the social worker found a women's support group for her. Sally had made the mistake of dwelling obsessively on her marital problems with her colleagues and even her boss at work. Her boss finally told her to keep her troubles at home or lose her job. Unfortunately, Sally was simply going through the common cycles seen among depressed, suicidal clients.

The typical phases of reactive depression such as Sally's in the preceding case example look like the diagram in Figure 3-1. A precipitating event such as the loss of a loved one, a job, money, status, health, or something else of major importance to an individual occurs. The person becomes sad, despairing, and perhaps suicidal. This state turns into an even worse state of lethargy, hopelessness, and

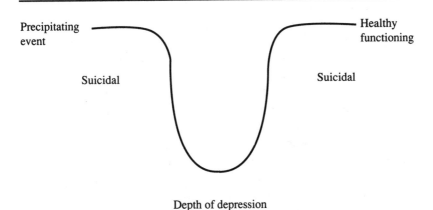

Depth of depression

Figure 3-1. The depression curve.

utter despair. At this bottom point the patient tends to be less actively suicidal, if only because of being too lethargic and lacking in physical or psychic energy to commit suicide. Gradually as the person improves, his or her energy comes back, often revitalized by anger at whatever or whomever had precipitated the depression. This is an unstable, erratic period that once again brings out suicidal tendencies as the developing anger occasionally is turned inward (leading to self-blame and guilt) and then outward again.

Social support intervention is best initiated soon after the occurrence of the event that precipitated the depression. By encouraging free discussion and ventilation of the hurt, anger, and developing feeling of despair, the worker minimizes the likelihood that it will become overly internalized and self-blaming. Depression involves both cognitive and emotional components, and both must be addressed to help guide the person safely, informatively, and therapeutically through the whole cycle of ventilation, assessment, clarification, planning, and restructuring. The planning phase was difficult for Sally because she was not only financially but also psychologically dependent on a husband who was not providing her with the emotional support she needed. The poor self-esteem that she had to begin with was worsened by her angry husband, who had major problems of his own that he completely denied.

The plan for Sally therefore involved her interacting more with those in her system who were constructive and supportive, primarily her parents and her daughter. She also joined a support group of women who could relate to the same issues. These group members were extremely supportive, and several became Sally's close friends and confidants.

The treatment of major depression must involve social support development. Various estimates exist for the prevalence of depressive disorders, but it is generally accepted that from 9 to 26 percent of all females and 5 to 12 percent of all males have clinically defined depressive disorders at some time in their lives. Furthermore, the incidence of these disorders appears to be on the rise in people who grew up after World War II (American Psychiatric Association, 1987). Depression is among the most common problems seen by social workers in practice and one that is directly relevant to social support. Severely depressed people often tend to isolate themselves from others and often seem to feel guilty, embarrassed, or ashamed. They cut themselves off from friends and loved ones, thus exacerbating the condition. Their withdrawal then becomes more pronounced as former members of their support system disengage and the depression deepens.

For major depressions and dysthymia (chronic depressed mood for at least two years), biological markers and individual and family histories of depression are usually present. Biochemical changes develop and worsen as the disorder runs its course. For those more debilitating depressive disorders, medications are required using tricyclic antidepressants such as Elavil (amitriptyline) and Tofranil (imipramine) or Prozac or even the MAO inhibitors or, in the case of bipolar (manic depressive) disorders, lithium is occasionally required. Most social workers accept such psychopharmacologic interventions as needed and useful complements to psychotherapeutic interventions but only in the case of major depression. Research in pharmaco-therapy has been mixed (Beck, Hollow, Young, Bedrosian, & Budenz, 1985), and either cognitive therapy or antidepressant drug intervention can successfully alleviate symptoms, although combining the two seems not to make any significant difference (Murphy, Mimons, Wetzel, & Lustman, 1984). But whether or not medication is used and whether the depression is minor and reactive or major and ingrained, an inevitable consequence is the cutting off of social supports and a subsequent needed response by the social worker to reverse that process.

Questions

1. What do you see as the major impediments to using social support interventions in your own practice? Consider practical as well as theoretical issues. How could you overcome those obstacles?

2. Develop a brief case scenario for each of the five problems in using social support: (1) faulty perceptions of reality, (2) parataxic distortion and low self-esteem, (3) depression, (4) individuality of need, and (5) deficient social skills.

3. Describe how you might change your approach with a depressed client who repeatedly fails to connect with the activities and/or social supports that you recommend and attempt to include. Be specific in describing clear, concrete, *manageable* incremental steps toward developing a social support system.

References

American Psychiatric Association. (1987). *Diagnostic and statistical manual of mental disorders* (3rd ed., rev.). Washington, DC.: Author.

Beck, A. T., Hollow, S., Young, J. E., Bedrosian, R. C., & Budenz, D. (1985). Treatment of depression with cognitive therapy and amitriptyline. *Archives of General Psychiatry, 42* (Feb.), 142–148.

Burns, D. D. (1978). *Feeling good: The new mood therapy.* New York: Signet.

Fischer, D., Godd, B. A., Nadler, A., & Chinsky, J. M. (1988). Social psychological influences in help seeking and support from peers. In B. Gottlieb (Ed.), *Marshalling social support: Formats, processes and effects.* Newbury Park, CA: Sage.

Lakey, B., & Heller, K. (1988). Social support from a friend, perceived support, and social problem solving. *American Journal of Community Psychology, 16*(6), 811–824.

Murphy, G. E., Mimons, A. D., Wetzel, R. D., & Lustman, P. J. (1984). Cognitive therapy and pharmacotherapy: Singly and together in the treatment of depression. *Archives of General Psychiatry, 41*(Jan.), 33–41.

Nadler, A. (1986). Self-esteem and the seeking and receiving of help: Theoretical and empirical perspectives. In B. Maher (Ed.), *Progress in experimental personality research* (Vol. 14). Orlando, FL: Academic Press.

Pearson, R. E. (1990). *Counseling and social support: Perspectives and practice.* Newbury Park, CA: Sage.

Wright, J., & Beck, A. T. (1983). Cognitive therapy of depression: Theory and practice. *Hospital and Community Psychiatry, 34*(12), 1119–1127.

Yalom, I. (1985). *Theory and practice of group psychotherapy* (3rd ed.). New York: Basic Books.

Chapter 4

Marriage and Social Support

Marriage and the Mental Health of Men and Women

Men and women marry for many different reasons, but generally factors such as having companionship or a trusted individual to talk to and care about are high on the list. Other important issues are social and economic security, status, and sexual needs. Whatever the reasons for entering into marriage, it is the strongest bond by which two people can commit themselves to one another. Even today when half of all marriages in the United States end in divorce, marriage is still generally entered into with the intent of forming a strong, intimate, and permanent bond that no other relationship can supersede.

An old joke—"Marriage is a wonderful institution, but who wants to live in an institution?"—seems to reflect the ambivalent feelings and even the apparently contradictory research findings that often relate to marriage. It does seem to be a helpful and supportive state—at least at sometimes and for some people but not at all times for all people.

In the past 30 years, there has been a decided increase in long-term relationships that do not follow the traditional definitions of marriage or family. Today, couples of the same sex make lasting commitments and often choose to raise children. Communities vary considerably in their responses to and level of support for such unions. Large urban areas and more liberal communities are generally more accepting of such nontraditional couples. This greater acceptance, when combined with the practical and economic advantages of people's combining resources, has recently found an additional significant reason for monogamous, enduring relationships, namely, AIDS.

AIDS and a variety of other sexually transmitted diseases have radically altered the sexual behavior of heterosexuals and homosexuals alike. It has become potentially dangerous to people's physical health to have multiple sexual partners. In addition to physical safety, monogamy also includes the significant advantage of a consistent social support system that provides a reasonably safe, caring, supportive relationship in the form of a single partner. It is clear why many people opt for commitment to a single partner—homosexual or heterosexual, with or without a formal marriage, with or without children. It is more accurate in recent years, therefore, to view "marriage" in a broader context, to include various enduring relationships, rather than to see it only in the more traditional sense.

Jesse Bernard (1972), in her early book entitled *The Future of Marriage,* first gathered and described several research projects that noted the discrepancies between men and women in relation to their experience of marriage. She concluded that marriage is a supportive and protective arrangement for men but not necessarily for women. Citing numerous previous studies, she reported that the overall mental health of married men, operationally defined in several ways in different studies, seems to be superior to that of single men, whereas married women are actually less healthy mentally than are single women. Bernard knew that many would argue that this difference, at least for men, was due to the initial "superiority of the sample" (meaning that "mentally healthier" men get married, whereas single men are less "mentally healthy" to begin with), thus accounting for the ultimate differences between the two. She corrected for this initial-superiority factor by methodologically holding constant and comparing male populations that were equal on the basis of age, race, education, and so forth. Even after this, she found that married men were mentally healthier, therefore concluding that it was in reality the fact of being married, not the initial superiority, that accounted for the benefits to men.

Gender, Roles, and Expectations

Historically, roles have been defined by gender within marriage. Women stayed at home, raised the children, took care of cooking, housecleaning, and other household and familial chores. Men worked outside the home earning money for food, clothing, housing, and other necessities for the family. Furthermore, the husband expected more nurturance, emotional support, and affection from his wife than he was required to provide her. She was expected to provide this support and affection, but if he gave it to her, he was considered to be exceeding his required role tasks as a husband.

Some believe that the differences in how men and women are raised in our society are the result of role expectations from very early in life (Lewis, 1976). Males have been expected, as young boys, to be more aggressive and competitive in order to be able to earn a good living later in life. They have been told, as young boys, to give up their needs for affection, which are viewed as more feminine. These needs cannot be erased, so men develop more guilt, which comes out in the form of compulsions or obsessions, which are rather repressed, guilt-related phenomena. When these feelings do manifest themselves, they tend to translate behaviorally into deviant, outwardly oriented behaviors.

As discussed in the next subsection, Scarf (1980) speculated that women have higher rates of depression than men because they are expected to be the more feeling, emotional gender. Some feminist research and literature have also upheld the view that women take on an unfair, added societal burden as a result of the tendency that they, more than men, have to blame themselves when things go wrong. This problem is often compounded by the fact that men also frequently blame women when things do not go well. Within marriage this creates problems for women but not for men. Men can pass the "blame" onto their wives, and the wives have been socialized to accept it. One can easily see why rates of depression are higher for married women than for single women, and, at least according to some studies, lower for married men than for single men. The fact is that married men can deny their own role in family problems and project the blame and guilt onto their wives, who probably assumed the problems were their "fault" to begin with.

Women, on the other hand, have been encouraged since early childhood to cultivate an affectionate nature. However, the male-dominated society, having gained more actual power through its aggressiveness, devalues this affection. Thus, women are more frequently depressed because of having been socialized as individuals who care for and nurture others, and therefore who become more dependent themselves on such interactional needs. Rejection or loss for a woman is not only a more profound blow to the ego or self-image (or whatever one may wish to call it), but it is doubly harmful in that women internalize it or blame themselves rather than men (Lewis, 1981).

In a chapter entitled "Madness in Women," Lewis (1981) explained that women's mental illnesses are more likely to be exaggerations of everyday feelings than men's disorders (such as sexual perversions and obsessional neurosis), which more often involve bizarre transformations of the world or of the self. What are more commonly women's disorders, such as depression, more often involve a malfunction of the self and of the woman's connection to another. Lewis sees men's disorders as more likely to be exploitative and women's as having to do with affectionateness. "Women are not pushed to give up their affectionateness. On the contrary, as childbearers they are expected to cultivate it, only to discover that affectionateness is actually devalued by our society, however much of it is hypocritically praised. Women thus become ashamed of their own loving feelings, which actually do not count for much on the marketplace. And, by a process that is not altogether clear, the chronic state of shame is transformed into depressive illness or into one of the hysterias" (Lewis, 1981, p. 209). She goes on to say that most research also finds women to be more "people oriented" than men and that men are consistently found to be more aggressive than women.

The following quotation highlights developments from recent decades that have added to the discussion of roles and expectations, especially of women.

> Between the 1950s and the 1980s an old system characterized by little cohabitation, early marriage, high fertility, low divorce, continous employment by men until a late retirement, intermittent employment by females, and sex-segregated jobs has given way to a new system. The new system has higher rates of premarital sex, out of wedlock births, and cohabitation, later marriage, lower fertility, more divorce, early retirement by men, more continuous employment by women, and—just recently discernible—desegregation of jobs and lowering of the sex gap in pay. Yet common to both systems is the assumption that child rearing, housework, and emotional work will be undertaken primarily by women (England & Farkas, 1986, p. 20).

This dramatic and relatively sudden shift in marital and familial responsibilities has not been easy psychologically for women, who have simply been required to add the responsibility of breadwinner to their roles as wives or lovers and mothers. For many, these multiple, demanding roles have caused a high degree of stress and subsequent inability to cope. In fact, it has been suggested to modern women that society gives them three roles: wife, mother, and workers, but that realistically they can only expect to do well in two of those roles at any given time.

Relative Rates of Mental Illness in Men and Women

The relative rates of different types of psychopathology for men and women vary somewhat in epidemiological studies (Neugebauer, Dohrenwend, & Dohrenwend, 1980). However, rather consistent trends become evident after deleting the old studies, the methodologically weaker ones, and those that do not really sample a random and representative population. Of those remaining, most studies indicate a higher rate of affective psychoses for women than for men, with no clear rate differences for schizophrenics. There is also a very clear difference for rates of neurosis, with women having much higher prevalence rates than men have. However, men have a significantly higher rate of personality disorders than women do. These two trends hold true for several studies in various countries and at statistically significant rates, so the differences appear to be real, not merely subtle variations that might be explained through differences in definitions of disorders (Lewis, 1976). Furthermore, the size of the differences between the sexes is large enough with respect to these two disorders that even if the validity of some diagnoses is challenged, there would still be major differences. Compared with men, women have, on average, greater than twice the rate of neurosis. Men have significantly higher rates of antisocial and addictive types of personality disorders, and these studies probably underestimate their prevalence due to the fact that many men with these problems are not counted because they are in prisons or other institutions.

Among other perspectives on social support, it can also be viewed as something akin to group pressure to conform. If a person belongs to a social support system of friends, then he or she will be more likely to maintain the standards of behavior or traditions considered acceptable by that system or group—which has both positive and negative effects. On the positive side, there is considerable comfort in having clear guidelines for behavior and standard routines for getting up, eating, going to bed, and so forth. Routine and consistency in life, combined with clear guidelines as to expectations and norms of behavior, mitigate negative effects of stress. In relationships between two people, certain implicit as well as explicit norms develop over time, and these are somewhat unique for each couple. A husband may know, for instance, that his wife does not mind if he occasionally stays out late as long as he is only with other males, he does not drink to excess, he does not spend too much money, and he does not wake her or the children when he comes home. The husband knows that he will receive comfort and support from his spouse as long as he conforms to these generally understood norms.

On the negative side, there can be a fear or anxiety that lack of conformity to the expectations and norms of the support system will lead to rejection. If there is a felt problem in meeting the norms (for example, if the friend or spouse states or implies that a man will be rejected if he drinks to excess or gets involved with a female and he has difficulty with that norm), a person will be anxious and fearful. The fear of rejection therefore leads to anxiety at perhaps being unable to meet those norms and therefore possibly being cut off from the real source of support.

Many clinicians and researchers have tried to understand the consistent difference in male and female rates of psychiatric disorders. No matter how the data are collected, the rate of depression for women is higher than the rate for men. In her fascinating book about women's lives, Scarf (1980) focused on depression and why it is so much more prevalent among women. She says that in virtually every study— even when such factors as social class, economic conditions, and age are controlled for—women account for anywhere from two to six times the rate of depression for men.

Scarf (1980) discussed this matter with the late Marcia Guttentag of Harvard's Project on Women and Mental Health, who helped shed some light on it by pointing out a curious discovery she had made. In doing a content analysis of popular magazine topics for men and women, Guttentag had found that loss was a significant theme in the stories written for women, whereas adventure and the overcoming of obstacles were dominant themes in material written primarily for men. Women were often written in to male-market articles as objects of fantasy, sometimes along with other elements that were considered issues to be mastered. Furthermore, the articles for women often discussed how to deal emotionally with others, and particularly how to please men. Guttentag indicated that the female mass market was preoccupied with the issues of disruptions in relationships or crucial bonds. The issue of loss even extended to concerns over women's loss of their attractiveness or effectiveness. Essentially these articles seemed to indicate that women are more sensitive to losses, particularly in relationships.

Another view of women and depression is offered by Phyllis Chesler (1972) in *Women and Madness*. She views the consistently higher rates of depression for females as being the result of a hostile, male-dominated psychiatric profession that punishes women by labeling them depressed. She feels that the label of depression is a covert societal mechanism that men use against women who do not accept their roles as inferior. Although Chesler makes some excellent points, her views are not well substantiated statistically.

According to Scarf (1980), there seem to be common depressive themes at each stage of life for women. In the teen years, females are typically preoccupied with the search for commitment and intimacy, while weighing these against the costs of careers. In their 30s many women already feel cheated by their mistakes or disillusioned that their girlhood dreams have not and possibly never will come true. In their 40s, or midlife, many women feel that they are losing identity-conferring roles (that of mother, for example, as their children leave home), which they perceived as their source of interpersonal meaning. It is also at this age that women often become concerned because their attractiveness, which is related to their sexual appeal to men, is fading, thus endangering their power in this male-dominated society. For some women, this can be a threat to their very emotional survival, especially when combined with the loss of their children as they grow up and leave home.

The Importance of the Issue of Relative Rates of Mental Illness

The issue of whether men or women have higher rates of certain types of mental illness is difficult to answer conclusively, yet too significant an issue just to ignore. Part of the reason it is so difficult to answer is that there are real distinctions between *incidence rates,* which refer to data collected on first admissions to hospitals or available statistics from treatment facilities, and *prevalence rates,* which refer to what is supposed to be the real or actual number of people with a disorder. In other words, "prevalence" refers to what truly prevails in any given society at a point in time. Also, in considering the accuracy of rates of depression for women and men, there are genuine concerns about diagnostic validity—that is, about whether a diagnosis such as that of depression describes the disorder clearly and consistently enough that it cannot be incorrectly used, and that it can be used for that disorder and no other. A third but related problem area is bias in diagnostic work. Diagnoses of hysteria in the past have almost invariably been applied to women, whereas certain "male" diagnoses have been invariably used for men but rarely for women. For instance, men are disproportionately viewed as having obsessions and compulsions as well as higher rates of alcoholism, drug addiction, and deviant sexual compulsions such as child molesting, rape, fetishisms, exhibitionism, voyeurism, transvestism, sadism, and masochism. Although these viewpoints may frequently reflect reality, they also may be self-perpetuating and lead to stereotypes related to gender.

Some of the problems related to the validity and reliability of diagnoses should diminish with the continuing revision of the *Diagnostic and Statistical Manual of Mental Disorders*—as of this writing in its third edition, revised (American Psychiatric Association, 1987). This book, considered by some to be the diagnostic bible of all the mental health professions, is much improved over earlier editions. Sexual, cultural, or age-related biases of the diagnostician should therefore be minimized, although they probably will not be completely eradicated. Future editions are expected to have greater input from social workers and other mental health specialists, which should help sensitize diagnostic procedures to real differences in the various disorders.

The issue of the real prevalence of depression in women and in men is also too important to be lost in political rhetoric. In any society some of the differences between men and women are based on biological and biochemical characteristics, and others on societal, political, and economic factors. The differences in the ways males and females are raised in our society also undoubtedly have major, lasting effects on goals, on expectations, on confidence levels or lack of confidence in certain academic or skill-related areas, and on their performance and aspirations in many other areas of life.

Following are two representative case examples concerning marriage and gender differences. In the first the focus is on a woman who takes too much responsibility for the marriage, and in the second the subject is a man who is neither responsible nor sensitive to the emotional needs of his wife or of others. Such examples run the risk of stereotyping people and situations, but they also demonstrate gender-related trends in behavior in marriage.

Self-blame and Self-esteem

Mary Beth was a 32-year-old married secretary with no children. She lived alone with her husband, having moved out of her parents' home when she got married. Her presenting problems were depression, loneliness, and a developing reliance on alcohol. She had recently separated from her husband, who had left her after a series of arguments over what she felt were superficial issues but which culminated in his telling her that he just did not think they were right for each other and that maybe they should call it quits.

"I don't know what I did wrong," she began. "I think it must be me—at least partly, because this has happened twice before. I do everything he wants, then the bastard leaves me."

Mary Beth's self-blame was misplaced, particularly as she described the circumstances of her recent separation. Her history required several sessions relevant to her relationship with her father, an alcoholic whose affection for her had been both caring and rejecting, and even viciously demeaning at times in her life. Being the adult child of an alcoholic (ACOA) put Mary Beth in a particularly demanding type of client category for social support intervention. ACOAs are often unable to trust or get emotionally close to someone else due to their histories of mercurial parental affection and/or of sudden inexplicable rounds of being berated or abused or neglected as children. Such histories do not lead easily to the ability to trust and to develop close bonds with another. Thus, ACOAs frequently find themselves desperately involved in emotional relationships only to back away when the solid, ongoing, difficult linkages begin to develop between two people based on trust.

Mary Beth had in fact chosen a man who "liked to drink a lot" and who became abusive toward her (once physically) when she dissatisfied him. Her self-esteem and image were based on his reaction to her. After Mary Beth read some books I gave her—for example, Children of Alcoholism *(Seixas & Youcha, 1985)—she joined an ACOA group, and we continued individual treatment as well.*

"Whenever I tried to get really close to him, he turned around and acted like a real rat. I guess they can't all be like that, can they?" she asked, with some expectation that I would answer. She really knew the answer. I began by helping her to see the strength of several of her other relationships, mostly with women that she knew from high school. We also discussed her capabilities at work and her developing sense of being a strong, attractive person who deserved more from a relationship. I encouraged her to recognize her own compliance in this process in that she chose poorly, misplaced her trust, and recoiled from genuine openness with trustworthy men because she couldn't get herself to let her guard down. Having recognized and discussed the pattern of choosing alcoholic, abusive men as a way of recreating her own "comfortable" but alienating and lonely life pattern, she reexamined what she wanted. Treatment involved not only recognizing the destructive pattern but of correcting it without undue guilt or

recrimination, two processes in which she used to engage regularly. Instead, we worked on her own self-esteem as a separate, good, healthy, autonomous individual, while further considering new relationships.

The new system of social support initially consisted of one close female friend and a sister. Gradually she became involved in a church group and a women's softball team. Eventually, her husband came back to find a woman who was evolving from being very "other-oriented" to one who recognized that although she did need and enjoy the company of others, her happiness and satisfaction had to come from within. She also made several appropriate demands on the husband concerning his drinking as well as his behavior and attitude toward her. When treatment ended, she had a large and healthy system of friends and had turned around the issue of responsibility in her marriage. Her husband, who was genuinely confused and dumbfounded by this change over a three-month period, was trying to redevelop the relationship with a new respect, admiration, and understanding for his wife.

As Mary Beth worked at redefining her self-worth, she recognized that even though others are important, she cannot rely completely for her sense of self-value on someone else, even on her husband. When a partner's own self-worth is based on demeaning others, as so often happens in abusive relationships, the results can be catastrophic. Mary Beth needed to build a support system of healthier, more autonomous individuals who could help her see her strengths as well as her weaknesses and develop her legitimate inner sense of self-worth as well as her ability to get support and feedback from others in a healthy way.

Social support interventionists cannot and should not work with individuals, families, couples, or any other social systems in ignorance of the political, social, and economic system. These all can and do profoundly affect people in ways that clinicians not only need to understand fully but also need to know how to use for the benefit of clients. However, efficient and effective interventions can be developed only if they are founded on hard data and unbiased studies. Interventions in social support systems and networks can proceed only after the clinician knows *what* the facts are and *why* they are as they are.

Infidelity and its Rewards

Bill, a successful 32-year-old building contractor of Greek descent, came in for treatment complaining of depression but also of a sense of being without goals or direction. Anna, his traditional, attractive wife of eight years, was 29 and wanted him to make more of a commitment to their life together partly by starting a family.

"I don't know what the problem is," he began. "I have an expensive, beautiful house, two fancy cars, and a business of my own, but I'm not happy. Anna's a good woman, and she looks good, too, but I'm not interested. Two nights ago I picked up a great-looking woman, and we made it in the front seat of my car. It was great, but I still feel like dirt."

Bill had a history of one-night stands and had recently been buying the services of different prostitutes. "I don't want a relationship. I want sex," he said on numerous occasions.

He was very good-looking but had a deformed left hand that had made him very self-conscious, at least as a youth, and some of his current behavior appeared to be related to his need to compensate for his poor self-esteem by getting women to become attracted to him. Bill admitted that he liked women to tell him how good-looking he was, but then after he slept with them he never called them back. This was strictly a game for him, to see if he could manipulate them. It was also his way of getting out a great deal of repressed anger toward women.

However, Bill had come to a stage in life where his wife, his age, and other life circumstances required that he either settle down and make a commitment or leave his wife. Anna had said that if he had a need for an occasional fling she would tolerate it, but this permission did little to alleviate his guilt.

Bill had few close friends but many acquaintances. One of his closest friends was a buddy from college who was also married but who likewise considered himself a ladies' man and who frequently went along with or helped set up trysts for Bill and himself.

After several sessions I became increasingly confrontational with Bill. He tried to present himself as a passive player in this game that he enjoyed, yet found ultimately unsatisfying. He said, for instance, that he and Anna had recently stopped using any form of birth control. He had already convinced himself that if she became pregnant he could still leave her, because he'd give her plenty of money and she had said that, whether or not they had a child, she would divorce him if that was what he wanted.

*In some ways Bill was going through an existential crisis,
questioning his real values and priorities in life. After much
discussion he recognized that the impressive material wealth he was
accumulating did not compensate for what he was missing in life,
namely, meaningful relationships, which he was trying to make up for
through one-night stands and ostentatious material goods. The
extremely busy, demanding work of owning and running his own
business did not leave him the time needed to develop and maintain a
good, open, trusting, communicative relationship with anyone, even
with his wife.*

*After encouraging Bill to ventilate and describe his concerns, I
took the risk of confronting him with several of his inconsistencies. He
said he passively went along with these women, who found him
attractive, and that he was just meeting their sexual needs and at the
same time his own. I pointed out that from what he had said, he was
using and degrading the women and himself in a tawdry game that he
had unwittingly stacked against himself. He said that Anna did not
really care whether he stayed or left, or whether they had children or
not. After making sure of my facts, I pointed out that his wife, who had
chosen to stop using birth control, was only responding to his
ambivalence and lack of commitment by appearing to be equally
noncommittal. In one joint session, she had indicated that much of her
behavior was due to pride and self-defense, both of which were
understandable; she feared that if she really let him know how much
she cared and depended on him and then he left her anyway, she
would be devastated. Finally, Bill said that his accumulation of cars
and a nice home made him happy. I again confronted him with the
fact that he was clearly not happy and that objects ultimately seemed
to do little to diminish his feelings of low self-esteem.*

*I gradually included his wife more in subsequent sessions and
helped them open the channels of communication much better. Bill's
admitted reliance on "quick fixes"—one-night stands, cold politeness
to his wife, and the use of material goods instead of a relationship—
were all gradually discussed and discarded as insufficient.*

Social support development in the case example just presented
essentially involved rebuilding the bond between husband and wife
and their very close extended family. When Bill complained that his
wife was cold, asexual, and disinterested in him and his work, I
supportively but directly confronted him with the fact that he was the
one who did most of the avoidance and who shunned open discussion

of genuine feelings. He avoided discussion of his fear of rejection by her or of his fear that she really "saw through him" and perceived him as the same very insecure, unattractive man that he really believed himself to be. To receive genuine understanding or love from his wife or anyone else, it was necessary for Bill to risk being open and honest himself, not manipulative and superficial. This was difficult and frightening for him, as it is for many other men who find open discussion of their own doubts, fears, and inadequacies to be so threatening.

As part of the process of social support system development, I encouraged Bill to talk more with his father, a traditional male from the old country who served as an excellent role model—in a negative way. That is, Bill could learn what not to do by observing his father. Bill did not relate to women openly because he had watched his father denigrate his mother since childhood. His parents barely tolerated each other for 35 years, and at some level Bill dreaded a similar fate. As he came to trust me and his wife, he confided more about those fears. He also joined a men's support group where for the first time in his life he experienced men talking with other men about their fears, their relationships with wives and lovers, their hopes and expectations, and other issues. Bill wanted to open up and deal with such issues but had never been taught how to do so. His slow, gradual learning to confide in me, then in his wife, and then in the support group led to much deeper levels of trust and openness within his marriage.

The bond of a close relationship in marriage necessitates major risk taking, because for the husband it involves letting his wife know of these fears and saying openly that the facade that many men maintain is a cover-up. The alternative of maintaining a more traditional macho stance frequently leads to alienation and isolation from self and from others—which is clearly the antithesis of the development of a social support system. Few men have a role model for openness in their fathers, but there is growing hope and belief that they will learn to value openness, communication, and affection in the same way that women are more likely to do.

Bill's involvement with a men's support group was excellent for him because it provided an existing, structured social support system that had as its primary goal a better understanding of feelings and relationships. The group was composed of men who felt that they needed to change their behavior and feelings toward others, but particularly toward women. Most of them were divorced and recognized that they needed help in opening up emotionally and trusting others. Through this support system Bill had the opportunity to relate to and observe other men to whom masculinity meant being tough, cold, avoidant of feelings, sexually manipulative, and more interested in power than in balanced relationships. These supposed masculine attributes, which are invariably counterproductive to the development of meaningful relationships, cause a crisis for many men in their 30s—a time of life when the significance of meaningful relationships and family social supports becomes focal.

Key Questions and Their Use in Marital Work

Among the most common clients in social work practice is the depressed man or woman caught in an unhappy marriage with an insensitive, unaffectionate, domineering, or nonverbal husband or wife. The wife's complaint typically is that her husband simply does not care about her and the children; the husband often complains that he feels overwhelmed and unsupported. The spouse, either husband or wife, is considering divorce but hesitates because of financial concerns, the children, or uncertainty about whether or not he or she still loves the spouse.

When confronted with these common scenarios, the social worker needs to ask several key questions as the basis for further work in couples' therapy (Berg, 1988). The rest of this chapter examines four sets of questions that should be examined in marital work. It explains those questions and presents several case examples that explore them in more depth, using case management, network intervention, and support development.

1. What are the problems? Can they be limited to two or three specific issues?

The first session usually involves allowing the client just to ventilate and gradually to focus on specifics. In marital work, the social worker needs to guide the client toward specifics by asking clarifying questions such as these: "So your husband said he found you unattractive?" or "Your husband left and you do not know why at this point?"

These clarifying questions serve the purpose of gathering facts and history while alleviating some of the client's anxiety by helping him or her focus on and "name" the problem. The initial visit or two can become overwhelming and counterproductive if the client spends too much time in self-blame, guilt, embarrassment, and pervasive but poorly focused anger. These emotions need to be put into the context of clear, manageable problem statements that can then be understood and mastered.

Defining the Problem

Marie was a 24-year-old mother of three children, ages two, five, and six. She was on welfare, and her boyfriend, the father of her youngest child, did not want to marry her. He said she was "too lazy, fat, and no fun." Marie had finished high school and had one year of experience working at a nursery school for toddlers, a job she enjoyed.

Marie came to Family and Children's Social Services because her one good friend said it helped people with "all kinds of problems." By the end of the session, she and the social worker had established that she needed help in the following four areas:

1. *Finding a job. This was Marie's goal, because she wanted to be out of the house more and improving her standard of living. The problem was that she needed health insurance and child care. As she and the social worker discussed this concern, the social worker suggested getting in touch with a program run by the County Employment Office that provides job training, medical assistance, and child care for one year. The social worker called that agency, and Marie went to see a vocational counselor.*

2. *Finding friends and people with similar interests. Marie said that she did nothing but watch the children and that she was becoming increasingly angry and abusive toward them. She knew that this was not good for them or for herself, and believed that if she could occasionally talk with others and have a few friends, she might be less anxious and angry. The social worker helped her to contact a support group at the YWCA that met weekly. These evening sessions included child care. The group was composed primarily of single mothers and was led by a social worker who said that the topics for discussion were developed by the members and had covered issues such as dating, anger toward children, self-esteem, religion, and finances.*

3. *Helping her six-year-old son, a withdrawn child who has poor language skills and was far behind his peers in school. Marie*

felt that her son might be retarded. She was especially concerned about the possibility because she had used drugs extensively when she was pregnant with him. The social worker had Marie bring the boy to the agency's staff psychologist for more extensive testing and possible treatment or referral elsewhere.

4. *Continuing treatment on an individual basis. Marie herself was depressed and felt that as helpful as all of this was, she would never be independent and happy. The social worker agreed to see Marie in continued individual treatment on a weekly basis, explaining that she would help Marie manage the various supports and services provided to her and her son, but also would work with her as an individual.*

The worker's approach was psychosocial with a strong cognitive component to help bring about realistic responses to the depression. This approach also helped reinforce Marie's independence while at the same time recognizing that her self-esteem would be more greatly enhanced if she discussed her problems and concerns not only with the social worker but also with the members of her support group, the psychologist working with her son, and the vocational counselor at the County Employment Office. This type of multifaceted, aggressive approach to case management not only provides an effective and efficient means to achieve specific goals, but it also provides a support system of professionals and nonprofessionals who help, support, and guide the client in each area that had been a problem.

2. Whose problems are they? Does your spouse also see these as problems, or does he or she consider them your issues?

These are important determinations to make, and the social worker must help the client make clear distinctions between his or her own problems and those that belong to the spouse. Furthermore, if some problems or issues do belong to the spouse, the client must be helped to recognize that he or she has little or no ability to solve them. A frequent problem is spousal alcoholism or drug addiction in a codependent marriage. Typically, the wife comes in saying that her husband is an alcoholic (or, more likely, that he has a drinking problem), but that she feels if she were just more attentive or better looking or a better wife or mother, he would stop drinking. She blames herself for his problem and needs to be helped to recognize clearly that she neither caused the problem nor keeps it going in spite of what both she and the husband believe. The wife in such a situation needs a great deal of support and reality-based, factual clarification to see her husband's patterns of alcoholism, of blaming her, of denying his own problem or responsibility, and possibly of being unable to change regardless of what she does or does not do.

The codependent spouse collaborates with his or her partner through self-blame, and this only serves to perpetuate a myth. These destructive patterns are usually the re-creation of one's family of origin. They are difficult to treat in that people are only doing what they believe is "normal" or at least what is comfortable for them because it is a continuation of what they know. Alcoholics are typically adept at denial and projection, and their spouses often are codependents who have or develop low self-esteem and subsequent dependency on the alcoholic spouse. Social workers with such clients often are surprised to see decent, capable, attractive, caring people blame themselves for being abused, ignored, and threatened by dysfunctional spouses who are alcoholics or drug abusers. The partner needs help to recognize that the problem is not his or hers but the partner's, and that not only is the self-blame misdirected, but that he or she has little or no capacity to change or even help modify the spouse's problem.

Establishing Boundaries and Ownership

Peggy was a 43-year-old mother of two sons, ages 15 and 17. She had started a part-time job two years earlier in spite of the objections of her husband Ed, an electrician, who said no wife of his should work. Ed was verbally abusive to Peggy, and he denied that he was an alcoholic despite all the evidence to the contrary. Peggy's father was also an alcoholic, and he had abused Peggy's mother. Peggy had become increasingly depressed and came into treatment reluctantly after she overdosed on valium. She had been referred to the social worker by the physician who treated her in the emergency room.

Peggy was evasive at first, saying only that the overdose was just a "stupid mistake" and that she should not have done it. The social worker encouraged her to say more, because Peggy appeared to be very unhappy. Peggy slowly admitted that she felt worthless as a mother and wife. No matter how hard she tried, Ed criticized her. Furthermore, their 17-year-old son had recently been arrested for selling drugs at school. This boy was her "pride and joy," and for many years he had been the object of most of her affection and had given her a sense of self-fulfillment. Even though the boy had a long history of "pranks," as she called them, he had never been in serious trouble until now. His personality seemed to change about a year ago, however, and he became erratic, anxious, and increasingly threatening toward her. She felt that her son's apparent drug abuse and turning away from her was the last straw and that her life was no longer worth living if he was lost to her.

Peggy described her youngest son as being quiet and something of a loner who did very well in school and seemed to have a few good friends but no one close to him. She admitted that she had never had the same intense attachment to this son that she had to his brother, even though the younger son was well behaved and tried hard to please her.

As Peggy spoke more about her husband, her repressed anger became more evident. The social worker encouraged her to examine the issue of Ed's use of alcohol, his abuse toward her, how she felt she caused or deserved the abuse, and the real nature and severity of his problem. The social worker did not tell Peggy it was wrong to blame herself but instead helped her look at facts, circumstances that led to both drinking and abuse, and circumstances surrounding Ed's alcoholism. The social worker helped her to confront certain contradictions between her behavior and her feelings about her husband's drinking. For instance, Ed made her call his boss on the frequent Mondays that he was too "sick" to go to work. She regularly made excuses for him, saying he had the flu or a doctor's appointment. Peggy even made excuses to the neighbors, who noticed Ed being brought home late at night by the local police—who also had taken it upon themselves to take care of their old friend. As Peggy described how her husband often made her buy his liquor for him, she first became embarrassed, then angry at herself for letting herself be used and blamed.

Network intervention with the married couple as the focus was agreed upon, because Peggy quickly began to realize that she had a tremendous amount of rage pent up against her husband, and she felt that she would not express it in front of her sons. Furthermore, both boys were put into individual treatment—the older one for drug abuse and the younger one for depression, which he masked by presenting an outward image of extreme competence to cover up his feelings of rejection and low self-worth.

The husband reluctantly agreed to three sessions of two hours each. They were to include Peggy's mother and father, Ed's mother (his father had died), Peggy's brother, sister, and sister-in-law, and a couple who socialized with Peggy and Ed and who already knew all of the family's problems.

In the first session, the social worker explained and summarized the reasons for the session, even though all the members of this network were aware of the circumstances. She explained that Peggy had been depressed and had recently attempted suicide. The reasons seemed to be related to problems in the marriage, and particularly to Ed's drinking, but also to the problems with her older son, who had been arrested for selling drugs and was abusing them himself. The social worker also explained that the two boys would have been with them, but Peggy's preference was to get the network together to focus on the marriage as a separate issue.

Her husband immediately and angrily said that he had no drinking problem and that he came only because Peggy was "acting crazy lately" and had even begun starting fights with him for no reason.

Peggy's mother retorted, "It's about time. She's taken enough from you for 20 years. You're a bum and a boozer and I don't know why she put up with you for as long as she did." This reaction came as a surprise to everyone, because Peggy's mother was a rather passive woman who herself had tolerated a similar situation most of her life. However, Peggy and her mother had talked extensively for the two weeks before this first network session, and her mother finally told Peggy she simply would not let her daughter fall into the same horrible predicament that she had allowed herself to live in.

The social worker asked Peggy to tell the others what she felt about the marriage and recent events.

"I don't know what to think," Peggy began, "but I don't think it's all my fault. Maybe three weeks ago [immediately before the suicide attempt] I would have, but now I think Ed's got some problems too."

Ed interrupted Peggy, saying, "Look, if I knew this was just to get me, I'd never have come in. She's the one who tried to kill herself, not me."

"Okay" said the social worker, "for right now, let's just try to see what the situation is and try to work together to improve things. The social worker then addressed Ed's mother, who was known to be continuously supportive of Peggy. "We don't want to pick on your son or Peggy. Do you have some ideas about what's happening in the marriage?"

"Well, I don't think Myrna [Peggy's mother] is fair in calling Ed a boozer. But he does have a problem. [She motioned to her son not

*to interrupt.] He even had trouble in high school with drinking, but
we didn't think it was a big deal. I think it's been getting a lot worse. I
don't even call up there on weekends, even in the afternoon, because I
know he'll be drinking, and he just doesn't make much sense. I don't
think it's all Ed's fault either. Peggy's been kind of letting herself go in
the last few years—you know, she's just not as much fun or as
enthusiastic about the kids or anything, like she used to be."*

*That session continued with the social worker encouraging
everyone to express an opinion. By the third network session, the
consensus was that Ed definitely had a drinking problem even if he
continued to see it as minor. He agreed to talk with his Employee
Assistance Program Counselor at work, who was a recovering
alcoholic and someone Ed trusted. The second and third sessions had
involved a great deal of confrontation and clarification, with Peggy
receiving the support she needed to become confident and independent
enough to see that her husband's problems were his own. The boys
attended the last session, and they too agreed that their father drank
too much and was unfairly critical of their mother. The social worker
ended the network intervention sessions by affirming with the network
members that they could all help support each other, by acknowledging
Peggy's many previously unrecognized strengths and capabilities, by
stating that Ed is an alcoholic in spite of his continued questioning of
that assessment, and by assuring him that the network would be there
to help him, even though he alone was ultimately responsible for his
behavior and his drinking.*

3. What suggestions or ideas do you have for improving the situation?

The suggestions or solutions first proposed by the client tend to
be consistent with the misdirected self-blame. For instance, almost as
common as the codependent spouse of an alcoholic is the individual
who either wants to save or to change his or her spouse. Thus,
frequent initial comments by the client may be that the spouse had a
great deal of difficulty with trust or commitment because of having
been abused and neglected as a child. The client explains their having
gone into the marriage to give the spouse what he or she had never
had, expecting in return to receive love and gratitude. Sometimes the
client does not even require love in return so much as the knowledge
that he was the "knight in shining armor" or that she was the strong,
courageous woman who finally got her spouse to be warm and
sensitive, just as she knew he always could. Such scenarios are
common—and usually ill-fated.

The spouse who comes in for treatment individually because of marital problems tends to be the one willing to make the changes, sacrifices, or adaptations. This person is the one who feels to blame or responsible. The social worker needs to listen to the ideas and suggestions that generally involve the client's need to improve his or her efforts to change, save, or protect the spouse. Exploration of these alternatives needs to be encouraged, because these clients sincerely believe that they are responsible for their spouses' difficulties. If a social worker too quickly takes the action of directly or indirectly placing "blame" on the spouse, he or she will quickly lose the client's trust. The client will tend not only to be protective of the spouse but also deeply involved in denial.

Consciously and superficially, those clients see the marital problems as their own responsibility, and they will try to protect or save the spouse who may be seriously disturbed, alcoholic, abusing, unfaithful, or simply disinterested or disinclined to maintain the marriage. A client's efforts at changing himself or herself to alleviate such problems would be ultimately quite fruitless, except in instances where the client supports the spouse's dysfunctional behavior or is codependent. Clear, factual, and frequently confrontational, reality-based questions and discussions must ensue to help the client realistically recognize patterns of having tried and failed to save or protect the spouse in the past. As long as the client's suggestions for improvement are based on the premise that the fault is his or her own, however, no genuine improvement in the marriage can take place.

4. What has worked and what has not worked to improve the marriage?

Soon after the client has explored his or her past efforts or present intention of understanding the blame and responsibility, the social worker needs to address the likelihood of the success of such efforts. In all probability, the client has already tried hiding the alcoholic spouse's bottles, or tried becoming more attractive or sexier for the spouse who says he or she is no longer appealing. If these efforts have not worked, they can help the client see that the issues are the spouse's rather than the client's. Such experiences can help the client see that trying to maintain a marriage with someone who has a borderline personality disorder, who is highly manipulative, or who for some reason is incapable of forming close attachments can become a depressing practice in frustration. When the caring and love of the spouse is not reciprocated in spite of continued efforts, any spouse must reconsider whether the relationship is likely to change in the future.

Sometimes past efforts have achieved success. For example, codependent spouses who have at times become angry or frustrated enough to let the spouse take the consequences of his or her actions may have found that this led to some positive change in the abusive spouse and the marriage. Rather than picking the spouse up and putting them to bed or calling to work for the spouse with some story related to the flu, the client might be helped to see that such "saving" only makes the problem worse.

Developing a Plan

Albert was a 43-year-old school teacher whose second wife was 10 years younger than he. They had been married for slightly less than a year, and this marriage was marginally satisfactory to Albert. His new wife, Jo Ann, often complained that she'd been happier before they were married, when she'd lived on the West Coast. Albert had tried to change and to improve both himself and the marriage, but he was not sure how to do this other than to dress more stylishly or to listen to his wife's type of music. He also discouraged visits by his 10-year-old son from his previous marriage even though he had joint custody with his first wife, who lived nearby. Jo Ann in the meantime switched jobs twice as a substitute school teacher, finding both jobs very unsatisfactory and much less fulfilling than her previous positions in California.

These vague marital problems had come to an abrupt halt one day when Jo Ann announced that she was leaving Albert and that she never should have married him. She called him insensitive and said that he loved his son more than he loved her. She said that she did not hate him but also that she had never really loved him and felt it best to leave as quickly as possible to avoid further unhappiness. She moved out the next morning.

Albert's reaction vacillated the next few weeks. He felt anger, hurt, and confusion, and did not know who to "blame" but felt that something horrible must have caused this.

Jo Ann refused all further contact. When pressed, she laughed at him angrily and said he "sure was into denial." With help from several schoolteacher friends and the staff social worker at the school where he taught, Albert was able to face the reality of what had happened.

Jo Ann had a history of going with men for three months to a year and then of breaking off with them when the relationships became more intimate and committed. She had been married once before, for less than a year, and had been engaged four more times before finally marrying Albert. The only man she really seemed to have loved was an alcoholic, highly successful professional athlete who was abusive to her and who had had multiple affairs while they were engaged.

The school social worker, a personal friend of Albert, felt that it would be helpful and appropriate to work with him informally in developing a support system while also examining the reasons for the divorce. Albert's general tendency was to blame himself, feeling that he had probably not been affectionate enough or supportive enough for Jo Ann's needs.

The social worker encouraged Albert to look at this apparent lack of affection, partly because it was such an inadequate rationale for divorce in his case. Albert was helped to recognize that he had been fairly supportive and affectionate but that this was apparently not the problem in spite of what Jo Ann had said. He was helped to put together many pieces of information about Jo Ann's past that he had chosen to deny. For instance, she had told him that her father was an alcoholic and had hinted often about abuse, but neither she nor Albert had followed through in discussing it. Albert had noted that in their brief courtship and marriage Jo Ann seemed to become more responsive and affectionate only when he became angry or did something to her that he himself felt was vicious or abusive. He was not good at expressing anger or hostility, although she responded positively to it and negatively to his frequent expressions of affection.

The school social worker encouraged Albert to get together with his friends often. Most of them were other male schoolteachers who were extremely understanding and supportive and who had clearly seen what Albert had not. In fact, two of them confided that they never understood why Albert had married Jo Ann, because she was anorexic, cold, and insensitive toward him. His friends also mentioned that they saw her as being very tough and "street smart," whereas Albert idealized her as being sophisticated and intelligent.

Albert's many friends gradually and informally shared their observations with him. Several had noticed her inability to develop or maintain close ties to anyone. Her only friend was an obese woman who, like Jo Ann, had no other friends, had been abused by an alcoholic father, and was divorced two years ago from a quiet, withdrawn individual whom she bitterly blamed for being hostile and cruel to her.

This support system was informally developed with Albert's active consent, because he could tell by this time that his friends seemed able to see obvious characteristics in Jo Ann that he had denied. Previously if any of them had pointed out Jo Ann's anorexia, her history of breaking off relationships with men, her positive responses to abuse, or her street-smart toughness, he probably would have become angry at them and would have denied these obvious observations. Albert's confusion, anger, hurt, and feelings of rejection subsided as the support system members individually and collectively gave him the message that his only mistake had been in loving someone who was not able to return that love in a positive, caring, and affectionate relationship.

Albert's school social worker friend met with him over coffee twice weekly and encouraged and supported his efforts to—

- *Maintain an active social life with male and female friends.*

- *Continue discussions with friends who also knew Jo Ann and who confirmed that she was a decent but remote and confused individual who could not have been committed to Albert no matter what he did.*

- *Increase his involvement with his son, whom he had neglected during his second marriage in an ill-fated attempt to show Jo Ann that he loved her more.*

- *Keep up his involvement with a local tennis club that provided not only a healthy physical outlet for his aggression but also an opportunity to socialize with others.*

This is a case example where denial concerning a loved one makes it difficult to develop and implement needed changes. Frequently couples develop patterns of codependent or even abusive behavior toward each other that serve real but dysfunctional needs. These needs are strong, ingrained patterns from childhood, which were developed on the basis of how the client's parents treated him or her as a child, or on how the client observed his or her parents interact with each other. The preceding case example is fairly typical in that it involves a case where couples see what they want to see in a partner, not what truly exists. Patterns of relating for couples are sometimes difficult to change because the patterns are so much a part of the relationship or they meet such strong needs that the couple either cannot see the obvious, or, if they see it, have considerable difficulty changing it.

Despite being extremely common in modern society, divorce has effects that are devastating to men, women, and children. It typically requires two to four years to achieve a constructive resolution to the stress related to divorce (Weiss, 1975). Sprenkle (1988) has developed a useful approach for treating divorced clients that incorporates many of the elements suggested throughout this book. Sprenkle defines the following 10 dimensions that should be addressed in "divorce therapy":

1. Acceptance of the end of the marriage
2. Functional postdivorce relationship with the ex-spouse
3. Emotional adjustment
4. Cognitive adjustment (development of realistic understanding)
5. Social support and adjustment
6. Parental adjustment
7. Children's adjustment
8. Use of opportunities for learning and personal growth
9. Process and outcome of the legal settlement
10. General life adjustments and physical well-being

Divorce or the ending of any significant, ongoing, intimate relationship is invariably a painful process. Social support systems are extremely valuable for people ending such ties, because they help those individuals with the transition to life without their partner. Family and friends can also help them realistically and objectively examine the factors that led to the dissolution of the bond. Another important component of social support systems in this instance is that they help individuals realize that life goes on, that other significant people exist who care about them, and that there is hope for the future.

Questions

1. To what extent do you feel the "gender gap" is closing in terms of spousal expectations over the past 20 years? In other words, do you see any evidence that men are becoming more giving or caring as women become more independent and gain more economic and personal security in the work force?

2. For couples in which one spouse dominates the other and criticism is one-sided but accepted by the partner who is unfairly blamed, how can you get both to change? Be specific, remembering that both people often have a stake in maintaining the status quo, even though it has become dysfunctional.

3. What particular problems do homosexual couples have that are additional to or different from those of heterosexual couples?

4. Specifically describe two advantages and two disadvantages for couples who are closely attached to the extended family of one of the partners.

References

American Psychiatric Association. (1987). *Diagnostic and statistical manual of mental disorders* (3rd ed., rev.). Washington, DC: Author.

Berg, I. K. (1988). Couple therapy with one person or two. In E. W. Nunnally, C. S. Chilman, F. M. Cox (Eds.), *Troubled relationships*. Newbury Park, CA: Sage.

Bernard, J. (1972). *The future of marriage*. New York: Bantam.

Chesler, P. (1972). *Women and madness*. Garden City, NY: Doubleday.

England, P., Farkas, G. (1986). *Households, employment and gender: A social economic and demographic view*. New York: Aldine.

Lewis, H. (1976). *Psychic war in men and women*. New York: University Press.

Lewis, H. (1981). Madness in women. In E. Howell & M. Bayes (Eds.), *Women and mental health*. New York: Basic Books.

Neugebauer, R., Dohrenwend, B. P., & Dohrenwend, B. S. (1980). Formulation of hypotheses about the true prevalence of functional psychiatric disorders among adults in the U.S. In B. P. Dohrenwend (Ed.), *Mental illness in the United States: Epidemiological estimates*. New York: Praeger.

Scarf, M. (1980). *Unfinished business: Pressure points in the lives of women*. Garden City, NY: Doubleday.

Seixas, J., & Youcha, G. (1985). *Children of alcoholism: A survivor's manual.* New York: Crown.

Sprenkle, D. H. (1988). Treating issues related to divorce and separation. In E. W. Nunnally, C. S. Chilman, & F. M. Cox (Eds.), *Troubled relationships.* Newbury Park, CA: Sage.

Weiss, R. (1975). *Marital separation: Coping with the end of marriage and the transition to being single again.* New York: Bantam.

Chapter 5

The Family as a Social Support System

The Family, Health, and Mental Health

The foundation for mental health is invariably laid in the family. In his seminal work on social support, Caplan (1974) described the essential elements of the family group. They included sensitivity to and respect for the needs of all members and good communication. He noted that most mental health professionals repeatedly see individuals from families that were deficient in these areas. Major problems develop when an individual grows up in a family in which his or her idiosyncratic needs are not somehow met and in which the individual instead serves as an object of the needs and displacement of feelings by other family members. Furthermore, if the individual grows up with disordered family communication, subsequent relationships often tend to be distorted as well, because communication is the basis for any relationship.

The concepts enunciated by Caplan are also significant in terms of the development and maintenance of a social support system. If a person has not adequately developed a meaningful sense of autonomy that permits his or her personal and idiosyncratic wants and needs to be considered and then acted on within the social environment, then he or she has inherited a significant obstacle to growth. By having needs appropriately met as infants and children, people gradually learn to discriminate between themselves and their parents, between reality and fantasy, and between their own needs and those of others. A healthy family structure meets the new and developing needs of infants and children and provides feedback to the child indicating that he or she has worth. Furthermore, a healthy family system responds appropriately to the needs of the developing child. A hungry child is fed, a frightened child is comforted, and a child engaging in dangerous activities is instructed and given appropriate limits. The family is a social system that nurtures and instructs both directly and indirectly.

The family also serves as protection against negative forces in the environment. An infant or developing child is unaware of many potentially harmful factors in the environment and learns through experience as well as instruction or demonstration. Through the family, a child learns to learn. For instance, if he or she learns from the family that the world is a hospitable environment in which one can trust others, experiment with different behaviors, develop relationships, and talk openly of thoughts and feelings, then the child will have learned how to develop a social support system.

If, on the other hand, a young child is taught through family interaction that his or her needs and desires are inconsequential to others, that the open expression of thoughts, hopes, or fears is deserving of anger or lack of response, and that basically the world as initially presented to them through their parents is uncaring or even hostile, then the motivation or even the aptitude to develop a social support system is diminished. It is within the family system that one first learns how to make linkages, connections, or bonds with others. Successful bonding based on open and accurate communication leads to strong social support systems. The capacity to develop these systems in later life is invariably begun in the family system.

However, it is neither fair nor accurate to "blame" the family when this process does not come about. The old, traditional, and often inaccurate stereotype of psychoanalytic theory, which was the cornerstone of casework well into the 1970s, was that it distrusted the family. Traditionally trained social workers were likely to have learned, for instance, that schizophrenia was the result of psycho-pathological communication, double binding, or insufficient bonding between mother and child during infancy. Current research in the etiology of schizophrenia and other psychotic disorders does not preclude these as possible factors that may lead to more frequent or severe relapses, but they are no longer considered primary causes. Another stereotype that has been inaccurate for some time is the concept of the family as essentially consisting of an intact unit of a mother, a father, and their biological children. In fact, such "families" are in the minority in American culture today. A family can consist, for example, of a single parent with his or her child (biological, adopted, or foster), or two elderly men or women living together, or three or four generations of single or married individuals. The last section of this chapter elaborates on the definition of the family by the Commission on Families of the National Association of Social Workers (NASW) and presents guiding principles recommended by NASW for working with the tremendously diverse systems we now see as the family.

As new research in genetics and biochemistry removes the onus from parental behavior as being the sole cause of children's autism or schizophrenia, faith and hope in the family have been renewed. Families can and do serve as the first line of help for most troubled individuals. In families that lack the capacity to provide the needed responses, communication, or nurturance, the task of developing a family social support system is definitely more difficult.

Spiegel (1982) claims that all family therapies have in common three basic ideological assumptions: the systems approach, the structural approach, and the interdisciplinary approach. In relation to the systems approach, he says that most family therapists pay as much attention to the family as a system of interactive processes as they do to the individual or identified client. They assume that to help the individual, the family of which he or she is a member must change some of its rituals or habitual ways of doing things. If not, the client reverts to dysfunctional interacting. Furthermore, the family is likely to resist change in the individual member alone, because such change could throw off the balance, or homeostasis, of the family system. In social support system work, the structural and interdisciplinary approaches are also accepted, but the concept of the system is paramount. The individual is a product of his or her family, and that family and its dynamics are a product of the community, culture, and society in which it survives. Aspects of these multilevel components include biological and genetic factors as well.

The family system is affected by the neighborhood and by the degree of support or lack of it that the family receives. For instance, the family that has active ties to the local church, scouting groups, community leaders, and neighbors tends to be more comfortable and to have a stronger sense of its acceptance in the community than other families do. This acceptance, or the lack of it, affects children. If children and their parents are well integrated into the community system, they are more likely to receive from it ongoing support, guidance, confirmation of their worth, and healthy social outlets.

Effects of Children on a Marriage

Children affect their parents' marriage and in turn are affected by it. In a review on marital satisfaction and how children influence it, Rollins and Gelligan (1978) concluded that marital satisfaction decreases with the birth of the first child and that it is curvilinearly related to family stage, although the later upward swing in satisfaction is not as consistently supported as the initial drop in satisfaction among young parents. Some studies do not support the view of early parenthood as being a strain or even a crisis for many marriages (Hobbs & Cole, 1976), but others do (Campbell, Converse, & Rodgers, 1976). It seems that many young parents describe the early parental stage as being a more tense and anxious period than any other.

This sense of early parenthood as being a trying stage is understandable. Most young couples are going through the difficult, demanding, but frequently exhilarating and exciting early period of marriage—a period of getting used to each other and of developing a strong emotional bond and commitment. However, this is also a period when financial problems are difficult, partly because young couples as a rule simply have less income than older, more established couples, but also because they are still developing a system of paying bills and learning to live together as a couple and to stay within their budget. It is not surprising that, at least at first glance, there appear to be conflicting results in studies on the early stages of marriage. This is a complex stage full of great pleasure as well as frustration and pain.

Very young children are a source of tremendous joy and satisfaction, yet they are also extremely demanding, frustrating, and anxiety provoking. The same adorable little child who can so profoundly touch a parent's heart with a mere smile or word can also be the object of a great deal of anger or even rage, particularly for young parents who are already feeling a great deal of stress from other sources. And so the advent of parenthood often seems to diminish the level of satisfaction with the marriage for both men and women; nevertheless, parents very often report that they perceive their children as having a positive effect on their marriage.

When Hoffman and Manis (1978) asked respondents: "Do you feel children have brought you and your husband closer together or further apart?," most of the respondents indicated that they were brought closer together. Less well educated people were particularly positive with this response. When parents were asked how it was that their children had this effect, their primary response was that children give parents a shared task—that both work together for their child's welfare. "Sharing joys" was the response of 25 percent of the women to the same question; other common responses were that the children are a "part of us" or a "product of our love" or that the child physically resembles or represents the parents themselves.

Those who indicated that their children made them grow farther apart gave several reasons, the most often cited being that the children precluded their spending enough time together as a couple. Another reason was the belief that children bring out disagreements either about childrearing in general or about a particular child, and another was the wife's becoming so involved with the child that she has less time to be a wife to her husband. Variations in the way children affect marital satisfaction are possibly best explained by Christensen (1968), who concluded that the type of effect ultimately depends on whether the couple wanted and planned for the children: wanted children strengthen a marriage; unwanted children harm it.

Family Patterns of Coping

Families develop patterns of behavior based on their own unique needs and histories. A family's method of coping and responding is the result of its culture, socioeconomic status, historical context, and properties related to each individual member. At the risk of stereotyping, McGoldrick, Pearce, and Giordano (1982) showed how Mediterranean and Jewish families are more expressive and overtly emotional than Anglo-Saxon families, for instance. Long-forgotten histories of various ethnic groups in the United States still account for ways in which families handle various situations.

In families where the spouses are from different cultures and are thus accustomed to different styles of behavior, confusion and stress often develop as a result of misinterpreting actions. Thus, the Irish or English man married to a more expressive Italian or Jewish wife may emotionally withdraw from stressful situations and she, on the other hand, may expect and want a strong emotional response or indication of his sense of anger, fear, love, or anxiety. Such differences lead to hurt, anger, and stress unless adequately discussed. Many families gradually learn about each other and adapt. Some become polarized and can be helped only with sensitive intervention on the part of social workers or others who recognize and respect cultural diversity within families. The children in families where parents have radically different coping styles are often torn between their parents. They feel that they must choose between them, and, indeed, when the parents are polarized the children often *are* forced to make that choice.

A social worker who wants to work on developing a social support system for polarized families with incompatible coping responses still has three choices: network intervention, case management, or system development. The clinical family networking approach of Rueveni, Speck, and Attneave, which is described in chapter 2, is occasionally useful for major dysfunction when nothing else works. Case management is another option, particularly when each family member has specific, workable issues of his or her own and especially when enmeshment exists and/or when the children would be better served by separating more from, rather than by being brought back into, the family system. For instance, case management is preferable to network intervention or system development when working with families with older teenagers (age 16 or over) who need to become more autonomous, or when one or both parents have extremely poor prognoses and are psychologically or physically harmful to the children. System development is often a good choice for families, particularly in cases such as the one presented next.

Mike's Great Expectations

Mike was a 15-year-old boy referred to the social worker by his school counselor. Until seventh grade he had been at the top of his class and had generally been regarded by parents and teachers alike as the ideal student. He transferred to another, more demanding private school when his ambitious, upwardly mobile parents moved to an expensive new home. Mike's grades faltered there, and his parents became increasingly frustrated with and demanding of him over the next three years. The boy's grades and attitude were declining rapidly by the time the social worker saw him. In fact, he was failing three of his six courses and had just been suspended from school for truancy, which he had hidden from his parents. The final act that convinced his reluctant parents to seek help was Mike's suicide attempt, which actually happened soon after his initial visit with the social worker.

At the first session, Mike's parents both said they loved him but were extremely disappointed.

"Mike, your father and I know you can do it, but we've had it as far as school goes," his mother began. "You went from the top of your class to the bottom, and we give up." The social worker encouraged Mike to talk but had limited success. She realized later that she should have spoken to him alone to have provided more support and to have allowed him more ventilation. This became particularly evident after

she received the call from Mike's parents saying that their son had cut his wrists after his father caught him once again missing school. The social worker helped get Mike hospitalized, worked with the hospital social worker and psychiatrist, and then began working with Mike and his family in system development after he was released from the psychiatric unit at the hospital.

In the first session after Mike was released from the hospital, the social worker encouraged him to talk about the reasons for the hospitalization as well as about what had happened there. (The social worker knew that the hospital social worker had worked with Mike in getting him to open up and trust and deal with his feelings rather than denying and repressing them.) Mike still had a great deal of difficulty expressing his feelings, although he now knew intellectually that he at least had to try. He and his parents recognized that his suicide attempt and his previous academic failures were clearly related to his anger at them and disappointment with himself. His hard-driving parents had pressured him to succeed and when he began to realize that he could not always be the best at everything, his own perfectionism rather quickly made him feel like a complete failure. In the first few sessions the social worker helped Mike talk about his feeling that if he was not a great success, he was automatically a great failure—both in his own eyes and in the eyes of his parents. This ventilation period was not only therapeutic and cathartic, it was also immeasurably helpful diagnostically.

The assessment phase included the parents, primarily the father. Mike's mother was a rigid, alcoholic lawyer who dealt with much of her own anger at her husband by taking it out on her son. She also had cancer and she, like her son, had tried to keep this knowledge from everyone until it became obvious. The social worker got Mike and his parents to talk about their expectations of each other. Separate sessions with the parents were required to help them realize that the pressure they put on Mike was having the opposite effect, that is, it made him feel more like a failure because he could never live up to their expectations.

During the assessment, Mike and his parents also did network diagrams. Mike's was particularly sparse because he was so rigid, perfectionistic, and depressed. He basically said that the kids at school were all jerks and that he disliked them as much as they disliked him.

The parents' diagram indicated that their social life was also very limited and that it consisted only of their immediate family or business contacts. The parents had initially spoken of a great deal of socializing among family and friends, but the assessment phase graphically demonstrated that none of them, parents or child, had any genuinely close friends with whom they could speak confidentially about personal or emotional issues.

Clarification involved further discussions of this rather meager social support system, but it also took into consideration the reasons for its paucity. The father began one session saying, "You know, I can see why Mike became so desperate. Ruth [his wife] and I don't even talk honestly with each other, let alone with friends or other relatives. We both work hard on our careers, and we've told Mike that to succeed you have to beat everyone else and that failure is a disgrace."

Ruth somewhat disagreed. "Wait a minute. We can't blame ourselves for what Mike is. We only want what's best for him, and I don't think we demanded anything he couldn't produce. We love him, so it's hard for us to watch this bright boy of ours wasting his life by failing in school. Somehow he's got to shape up. I don't think it's fair for us to be blamed for Mike's failing in school or trying to hurt himself."

The social worker joined in and supported Mike in clarifying his feelings. "I know you two care but you expect too much. Maybe I'm just average. I don't know. You always yell at me when I get bad grades, so I just hide the grades or ditch school."

Mike's avoidance, denial, and repression were major issues, because they had been well learned in his family. In addition to his parents both being social isolates, his mother adamantly refused to discuss her cancer in front of Mike. The social worker explained in separate sessions with her that by avoiding the frightful topic, she was modeling the same behaviors that had gotten her son into trouble, namely, denial, repression, and avoidance. "Look," Ruth said, "if I let Bob [her husband] and Mike know how scared I really am, those two would fall apart. I know who the really strong one is in the family. It's me. Bob would still be counseling kids like you do instead of running a successful company of his own if it weren't for me. I know you mean well, but if you and Bob keep on babying Mike, he's only going to get worse."

This session and two subsequent sessions alone with Ruth were essential in getting her to understand the development of Mike's problems. Ruth was drinking more than ever to cover up her understandable fear of cancer, which was potentially killing her. Her own father was an alcoholic, and she learned to avoid, deny, and repress feelings, often by throwing herself into work. The social worker helped Ruth understand that Mike's condition had deteriorated over the past few years precisely because he did the same things she did. As he covered up his failing grades and diminishing confidence, his depression and anger toward his parents grew. He was not allowed to express that anger or his personal disappointment, so he withdrew socially from peers and family and psychologically from his own repressed fears.

Ruth's cancer was a final blow. No one in the family really talked about it, and what emotions the family could deal with were all channeled into focusing on Mike as the family's failure to achieve. Mike had finally tried to kill himself (or at least to display his extreme despair) as one last effort to avoid his parents' constant anger and disapproval. It also was an expression of his belief that he could never be as "successful" as they wanted him to be.

The planning phase of treatment required that all the members of the family examine their past behaviors and realize a need to change. This phase was made easier for Mike, because his parents by that time had clearly and finally agreed that they loved him no matter how well or poorly he did in school. Much of the pressure was in fact internalized by Mike, and he needed to talk about the pressure he placed on himself as a way of relieving that stress.

Bob had made a concentrated effort to talk more with his son, and with some limited success, but it was clear that he was uncomfortable hearing Mike's fears. It was difficult for him to stop telling his son what to do. The social worker encouraged them to keep on talking, but also sensitively reminded them of a fairly elderly neighbor whom all three had mentioned in their network diagrams. The gentleman was respected by Mike and his parents and, because he was a reasonably successful businessman himself (and therefore respected by Bob and Ruth), he was asked to talk casually with Mike. This 70-year-old man's five children had all moved away, and he now welcomed these discussions with Mike. All agreed that these talks should be encouraged as a healthy social and emotional outlet for Mike. In fact, Mike had included him in his social network diagram as a close friend, much to everyone's surprise. Apparently Mike had already had a couple of "heart-to-heart" conversations with this grandfatherly widower.

One of the other major successes of this planning phase occurred when Mike himself suggested that he have his teachers write a brief progress note each week. While the social worker was uncomfortable with the family's continued reliance upon academic achievement as a measure of success, she allowed it because Mike was actively taking part in the arrangement. He needed to become more active rather than passively blaming either himself or his parents for his real and imagined failures.

Restructuring involved getting Mike to come in for weekly sessions that focused on opening up and trusting. This work was needed to counterbalance the familial modeling of avoidance and denial. The worker helped Mike realize that the more he covered up both his feelings and his behavior (for example, by hiding report cards or avoiding school), the worse the situation became for him.

The social worker encouraged Mike to join the soccer team at school as well as the debate club. His parents paid to have two of his classmates help him with school subjects. Mike had suggested this as well, and the two tutors became closer friends with him.

Mike's behavior, feelings, and school performance all continued to fluctuate, corresponding to some extent with the course of his mother's cancer. Ruth was able to see that she needed to talk about her fears of death and other emotions for her own sake as well as for Mike's. She was also encouraged by the social worker to continue her involvement with her church, which became a great source of comfort for her and a significant part of the whole family's social support system.

During several later sessions, the social worker facilitated emotionally charged meetings where Ruth spoke of her fears and hopes for her son. Her alcohol consumption continued actively but erratically. Because she refused treatment for herself as being too threatening, success was only moderate in terms of her drinking, but was better than expected for dealing with such strong ingrained personality traits within a family system.

As can be seen in this example of system development for a family, the phases overlap and are revisited. Ventilation never really stops, and planning and restructuring are at least implicit from very early on.

Also, intractable roadblocks are occasionally encountered. In this example, the prognosis was limited because of Ruth's alcoholism and the related personality traits. Mike was learning his behavior from his mother, and the intervention at least served as a way of minimizing the damaging effects of such modeling.

When the case ended, Mike had become involved with several friends on the soccer team and looked forward to a trip with his grandfatherly neighbor. The neighbor "adopted" Mike in a way that was not threatening to the parents, adding an important dimension to

Mike's social support system by listening and giving noncritical
feedback in a way that neither Bob nor Ruth could comfortably
develop in a short time with their son.

Helping the Family Function as a Social Support System

Social workers and social scientists have written extensively
about the family and the substantial changes it has gone through over
the years. The result for some has been rather confusing as
professionals, journalists, and laypersons alike enter the debate about
whether these changes have been positive or negative adjustments or
necessary adaptations, or unfortunate failures.

However, most agree that living in a family provides an intense
and long-lasting opportunity to know others intimately and to work as
a part of a collective unit for the good of the system. Family members
learn that they must interact responsibly with others and learn to share
responsibilities.

In modern times the nature of professional services vis à vis the
family's historical responsibilities has been debated. A good example
is the issue of child care. Conservatives claim that child care,
particularly for the very young, must be handled in the family and
even by the mother. Indeed there is a large body of occasionally
conflicting research that questions the effects of child care on infants.
Some argue that in this and other instances the natural social support
system, meaning the traditional family, is the appropriate unit of care.
They contend that social workers and other professional caregivers
actually undermine the family's existence and significance in society
by usurping these traditional roles.

Another frequently cited example of an area where conservative
and liberal viewpoints often clash is education—particularly around
birth control, sex, or education about the transmission of diseases
such as AIDS. Conservatives advocate less of a professional role and
more familial responsibility in education. They claim that the family
should be allowed and encouraged to educate its own children about
such intimate issues in manners that suit its particular customs,
cultures, or religions.

Actually, few social workers disagree on either child care or
education. Most would argue that if all families were actually willing
and able to raise and nurture small children or to educate youngsters
about sex, there would be little need for their services. The problem is

not so much an issue of beliefs or ideology as it is of practical outcomes.

The "traditional" family, as has been already discussed, probably never existed. The notion of what a family is and how it functions or of even what duties it performs for its children has changed throughout history. Today, we are once again in a transition period. We as a society are attempting to define the family and what it does.

In terms of its functioning as a social support system, the family as a unit should be nurtured and developed. It makes no sense to use relatively expensive and time-consuming professional resources to compete with a potentially functional system. Social workers can and must attempt to work with and through the family, at least where children are involved. Thus, whenever feasible, intervention should be oriented toward developing and nurturing the family so that it can provide an adequate social support system to its members.

The claim by some that social workers usurp and therefore undermine family resources misstates the problem. The problem is that the family is undergoing a tremendous amount of stress and in some instances it cannot or will not provide the help or nurturance that its members need. In those cases other systems must be added or even used to replace the "traditional" family.

Today unwed teenage pregnancy is the norm rather than the exception in some communities, and addictions devastate entire neighborhoods. Not all families living under such conditions can realistically be expected to cope. Poor families and single-parent families with limited education and few opportunities for advancement often can barely provide food, clothing, and shelter, let alone sufficient guidance, love, and support. It is truly remarkable that many families do survive and cope under such adverse conditions, but in those instances where family systems are overwhelmed psychologically, economically, socially, and spiritually, the system needs to be linked up to a broader, more positive base of support. Such supports typically include, but are not limited to, three important sources: churches and the clergy, community organizations, and self-help groups.

Churches and Clergy

Churches and synagogues are a frequently overlooked resource for overwhelmed family systems. Clergy in recent years have often been well trained as counselors. Most schools of social work now include a number of priests, rabbis, ministers, and nuns. The old notion of these individuals as being rigid or dogmatic often proves to be an unfair stereotype; they do much the same type of work as social workers but add an important spiritual dimension. Hope is a necessary ingredient in the successful process of change. Whether one chooses to view it psychologically or spiritually is irrelevant. Spiritually it can be seen as a belief that a power greater than oneself is present and cares and will help those in need. One can also view it as a significant factor in motivation, which is a precursor to most successful psychological change processes.

Furthermore, involvement with the activities of parishes, churches, and synagogues can lead to relatively instantaneous, yet strong and positive supports. Youth groups, choirs, and innumerable small committees that have been developed to help local churches also serve to help their members. Not only do the activities help the individual who participates, but his or her family also becomes accepted into a larger social system. This acceptance provides positive self-image and status, and frequently brings with it nurturance, affection, altruistic outlets, and other benefits as well.

Community Organizations

The family that is involved in neighborhood Little League, Girl Scouts or Boy Scouts, soccer, swimming, football, dance recitals, and other such activities within the community has healthy social and physical outlets and social support. As with so many other observations about social support, it is not clear whether the correlation of such activities and better mental health is causal or not. We only know that youngsters who are actively involved in such activities are more likely to be less depressed and to have better self-esteem than those who are not involved (Maguire & Martz, in press). The same is true of the elderly: long life and health have been shown to be correlated to a variety of formal and informal networks within their communities and with friends and relatives (Lepman & Longino, 1982).

Self-help Groups

Families that are connected with self-help groups of one kind or another also broaden their base of support. Self-help groups may be formed primarily for political and social action, for consciousness raising, or for mutual aid and support, but whatever their goals, they also provide social interaction and generally some degree of support for families.

Some self-help groups, including the following, are specifically oriented to family concerns:

- Parents Anonymous, which helps parents who have been abusive toward their children.
- Lamplighters, which supports parents whose children have died.
- Alanon, which helps family members of alcoholics.
- Alateen and Alatot, which help teenagers and young children in families where there is alcoholism.
- Parents Without Partners, for single parents.
- Families of Adult Mentally Ill (FAMI), for adults and other family members, such as siblings, who have a family member with an ongoing psychological disorder such as schizophrenia.

There are hundreds of self-help groups that directly or indirectly help families feel supported and needed while offering the families themselves an outlet for their own abilities and talents.

Contemporary Changes in Family Structure

The notion of what a family is has undergone many changes throughout history. There is current speculation that men and women maintain their more passionate feelings as a couple for only three years, that being about the time it takes to reproduce and wean an infant. Contrary to current Judeo–Christian norms, early men and women probably were not monogamous, or were only so while the woman was expecting, feeding, and caring for the infant. Much later, during the Middle Ages and through the Renaissance, children were treated as small adults and were sent out before the age of eight to work for others. They were not segregated from adults in the work-place or even the taverns. It was not until the 18th century, when some countries developed public schools, that children were separated from adults. With this development came the increase in the focus on the family and extended family as the unit of social support and nurturance.

The extended family became a great source of support in the United States for immigrant populations and rural families in particular. The agrarian society, which was dominant until the Great Depression, relied heavily on grandparents, aunts, uncles, cousins, and siblings not only to do farm chores but also to serve as school teachers, doctors, social workers, and in various other roles that are now highly professionalized. But the image of the "good old days" needs to be supplemented with data on the family. Even though divorce was relatively rare at the turn of the century, the chances were actually greater then that a child would not be living with either parent. For children born between 1911 and 1920, there was a 22 percent chance that at least one parent would die before the child reached 18 and a 5 percent chance that the parents would divorce. As health conditions improved and mortality rates declined, children born in the 1940s faced only a 20 percent likelihood of losing a parent through death or divorce. It was not until the 1960s the divorce rates took precedence over early parental death rates as the primary reason for children not growing up with both parents (Levitan & Belous, 1981).

In recent years the rate of change for the family has accelerated. More mothers now work outside the home than in the home for the first time in the history of the United States. That trend is unlikely to reverse itself in the near future, given the financial demands of society and the country's struggle to maintain its position in a global economy. The women's movement and feminism helped free women from the traditional, confining roles of mother and wife and opened up new opportunities that were not available 40 years ago. Yet, with these changes come stress and the need for other parts of the social system to change to meet the new reality.

Men have not adapted to the newer forms of family structure. To the surprise and disappointment of many who had both hoped for and anticipated a significant increase in male or paternal involvement with children, there is evidence that men have not changed. As discussed in chapter 4, women have simply added professional roles outside the home to their traditional maternal roles. When women have received help with child care in recent years, it usually has not been because the man in the home helped care for the child or children but because the woman paid for child care or got help from female relatives. England and Farkas (1986) maintain that if this trend continues, it is rather unlikely that there will be economic equality of men and women for some time. They make this claim based on the assumption that women's salaries are unlikely to equal men's as long as they must be responsible for most child care. Even if women's did equal men's salaries, women typically have custody of children after divorce, and this puts them at a disadvantage with regard to the likelihood of a second marriage. Women must combine increased earning power with demands for males to do more of the child care if there is to be not only economic equality but also equality and mutual respect and caring within the structure of the family.

The Need for Balance and Mutual Respect in the Family Structure

Social support within the family structure requires balance among the members. The entire family becomes more empowered when there is a more equitable sharing of resources and responsibilities. A "healthy" family support system is characterized by mutual respect and common concern for all family members. Such caring and concern can only be maintained where there is reciprocity and balance within relationships. In a family where one member dominates others or denigrates their roles, the likelihood of mutual respect and caring is diminished; communication then declines, and the development of an open, caring social support system within the family is lessened.

Network analysts have studied related issues such as longevity of bonds and density or closeness. They have established that relationships between and among individuals can best be maintained if people give as well as receive in a reciprocal relationship and if that exchange is reasonably balanced and equal. In dating, for example, if a woman feels that a man is not giving her enough time, affection, praise, money, or whatever she feels is lacking, she will break off the relationship, as will a man, whether the other person in the relationship is a woman or a man. Friendships are also based on the balance of giving and taking, respect and reciprocity. This exchange theory forms the basis for love, marriage, and family cohesiveness. If a family is "unbalanced" in its exchanges (for example, if the male provides most or all of the financial resources, then denigrates the woman who stays at home to raise the children or who works outside of the home but for considerably less money), then the relationship will not last, or it will be very stressful. Within marriages and particularly where there are children, there are constraints on ending relationships. People generally cannot end their relationships with their own children with impunity. Thus, stress often arises in families with children as a result of an imbalance of affection or faulty or problematic shifts in social exchange.

A social support system exists within families when tasks such as child raising are shared, when economic resources are both provided and spent on an equal basis, and when all parties see the others as giving and taking in a balanced way. However, such perfect balance is rarely achieved. Men and women are not treated as equals on the job in the marketplace, nor do they share the same cultural and social pressures regarding child care responsibilities. What is needed to redress these seemingly intractable societal imbalances is a redistribution of respect, status, and power within the family's social system. For instance, if the woman is the primary breadwinner for the family and the man stays home to take more responsibility for child care, the couple must share a sense of these tasks as being of equal value.

The family's ability to function as a social support system is affected not only by balance and mutual respect, but also by a wide variety of cultural, social, and even economic forces. The ground-breaking work by McGoldrick, Pearce, and Giordano (1982) helped social workers recognize obvious differences related to ethnic and cultural norms. In some cultures, children are highly valued and form the real reason for the existence of families. In others, children are seen as unfortunate burdens or even accidents who get in the way of more important plans. Having children cannot help radically affecting a couple's relationship.

About the most common type of case that social workers see involves the results of an imbalanced social system within the family. Typically, social workers see single-parent females whose husbands or boyfriends have left them because of a more attractive woman or because they came to view them and the children as a burden. The boyfriend or husband initially found the woman he left attractive—that is, his equal or better on the basis of social exchange—and she had felt the same way about him. But then after the birth of their first child she stayed home and became less "fun," spontaneous, or otherwise attractive, as she tried to maintain the roles of both worker and mother, or simply as she tried to adapt to motherhood. If she failed, or could only maintain both roles or simply adapt to motherhood by becoming more "dependent" on him, he would see her as just draining him, not as making a contribution.

The Family Support System and Life-Stage Transitions

Socially, children can have a tremendous effect on the happiness and well-being of parents. The young adults who make a comfortable transition from single life to being a couple to being a family with a small child or children are often rewarded with a highly supportive social network. In fact, the social network configurations of individuals generally follow a fairly set pattern for those who adapt socially. The typical social network of single males and females is composed of mostly same-gender close friends, particularly for females. Adolescent and young adult males have mostly male adolescent friends, and adolescent females have mostly female adolescent friends. There is more of a tendency for females to maintain these close bonds with other females than to form such bonds with men in early adulthood.

A surprising homogeneity of social network patterns exists over the course of developmental life transitions. The type of bonding that follows life stages can be seen in the context of social support system development. People form friendships on the basis of mutual identification, common interests, and backgrounds. Thus, single people have more single friends, young married couples without children have more friends who are couples without children, and so on, which explains the changing patterns of networks and thus of social support systems as people enter different life stages and family transitions. As a result of such patterns, the social activities of young unmarried individuals, for example, frequently differ from those of married couples. And, in fact, this particular transition can be a difficult time for married couples if, for instance, the husband prefers going out with his male companions or the wife prefers the company of her former and occasionally still single female friends.

When couples have children, their interests as well as time commitments and constraints all change. Especially for couples with their first infant, there is often both a desire and a need to get to know other couples who are going through or have already gone through the same experience. Again, the bond of friendship based on mutual identification and common interests forms the basis for a social support system of similar couples. Some, but not all, of the older network configurations are left behind, and as this happens, priorities, goals, and past loyalties and bonds change.

Change and shifting support systems lead to stress. When viewed from the perspective of life-stage transitions, these changes become complex. People tend to seek others in similar life stages and circumstances, but this often requires change caused by breaking the bonds of some former friendships. For married couples, same-gender friendships can be the source of problems, and different-gender friendships can be perceived as threats to the marital relationship. In short, married men are not encouraged by wives to maintain ties to old girlfriends, nor are married women encouraged to stay in touch with former boyfriends, particularly if the men are still unmarried.

The family as a support system can therefore be viewed along the same basic continuum as typical adult life-stage transitions. Young single adults have social support systems of young single adults; their closest friends, particularly for females, are other females. Married couples gradually shift toward friendships with other married couples, and later, if the couple has children, seek out couples who also have children.

Divorce and Changes in Social Support Systems

In the case of divorce, these social support systems are often dramatically changed or simply destroyed. For many couples, the loss of the extended social support system is more traumatic than the loss of the spouse. In a divorce where there is a mutual agreement to nullify the marriage, both parties presumably expect positive outcomes. However, divorce invariably affects the larger social support system. For instance, formerly married couples with children are no longer easily accepted into the social support system composed of other married couples with children. The ex-husband or ex-wife is often subtly excluded because he or she no longer fits the family configuration of the other intact families. Furthermore, the now-single member may even be perceived as a threat to the marital bonds of the other system members or, at the very least, he or she throws off the gender balance and symmetry for the system.

Typically, the divorced individual finds that he or she has to build a new network, perhaps composed of some old friends who have remained loyal or who never married, or of new friends who are divorced or single. The presence of children tends to be a deciding factor in these new configurations of social support systems. Divorced women with children frequently find new social support systems among other women with children. These systems are strengthened not only by commonalities of gender, loss, and child-raising needs but also by emotional ties related to the trauma of divorce and often-shared economic concerns.

Change such as divorce invariably involves stress, and people often try to avoid such stress by re-creating old, familiar situations and structures. Sometimes this is a transitional stage in which social support intervention essentially involves the social worker's moving into the role of the lost family member. I worked with one family in which the 38-year-old father had left his wife of 16 years for a much younger woman. The wife was depressed and angry and took much of it out on her 14-year-old daughter, who was very much like her father. This daughter had been equally devastated by the abandonment of her father, but with the added burden of anger from her mother, she was unable to cope. In her attempt to find affection and support, she became involved with a drug dealer nearly her father's age who introduced her to a variety of drugs and abused her sexually. The mother brought her daughter in to see me after two previous therapists had given up. By then the mother wanted her daughter put away, either in a psychiatric hospital or in an institution for delinquent girls.

When I first met the daughter, Pam, she was overtly hostile. Most of her responses were one word only—yes or no. When I finally very sincerely empathized with the tremendous hurt, anger, and rejection she must have felt from virtually everyone she cared about in her life, she broke down. Even this was followed in a few sessions by highly suggestive behavior and attire, which were all clearly and unambiguously rebuffed, with explanations that I cared for her as a good, worthwhile human being, not as an object of abuse and rejection. Once this phase passed, some obvious transference came into play. I was inevitably seen as the "good" father who loved and cared for his child because she was simply herself and worthy of love. Essentially, this young girl only needed the type of familial social support that was unavailable to her because of her mother's hurt and anger and her father's rejection. By appropriately using me as a temporary father surrogate, she was able to express her anger and distrust, but then to go on to indicate her need for affection, guidance, and support.

The mother also needed a great deal of help, even though she resisted almost as much as her daughter. By helping her to examine and then get past her anger at her rejecting husband who had so badly trampled her self-esteem and divorced her, she was able to rebuild her self-esteem. The mother could give nothing to her daughter as long as she felt so worthless herself. I served as a facilitator of the social supports within that family of two by stepping in where the father/husband had been. Furthermore, by just listening as well as providing encouragement, care, praise, and advice, I helped them rebuild their sense of worth. Without any sense of feeling worthwhile, one has little to offer in social exchange or support. As the mother and daughter developed a new and positive sense of who they were and how much they could mean to each other, they began to give each other the social supports so badly needed. I was able to leave this family after having temporarily provided social support and guidance and having served to build up the confidence level of its two members who in turn could help each other through the crisis and the blows to both of their self-images. The two of them had to learn to balance each other in a mutual exchange in which two people who value themselves in turn value each other. That is what a family's social support system does.

The Newly Reconstituted Family

Maureen was a 36-year-old legal secretary who had recently remarried. She had two sons, ages 14 and 16, by her previous marriage. Her second husband, Ray, a year younger than she, was not only very creative at his profession of carpentry but had also trained himself as an artist. Otherwise he was a traditional blue-collar worker who kept his artistic talents a secret from the rest of the world while Maureen enthusiastically encouraged his interests.

In fact, Maureen did nearly everything enthusiastically. It was her way of masking depression and poor self-esteem, which had originated with her distant and unaffectionate father. Maureen often "pushed" Ray to be more sensitive and outgoing, but her prodding had begun to have the opposite effect. Maureen persuaded her reluctant husband to come in to see me with her for several reasons.

"I love Ray very much, and I know he loves me, but he seems to be getting worse," she began. "He's sweet and sensitive and usually great with the boys, but every now and then he just withdraws and gets mean."

I asked Ray to tell me what he saw as the reason for their coming in for treatment.

"I don't think there's any real problem. I do love Maureen and the boys. Maybe I shouldn't back away from her the way I do sometimes, but I really need some peace and quiet myself. I don't think Tommy [the 16-year-old] likes me, and I know that Ken is a great kid, but he doesn't do anything, and I think he's got some real problems."

As we talked, it became clear that all four members of this reconstituted family had been withdrawing more in recent months. Tension was growing, the older boy was suspected of using drugs, and the younger boy was getting good grades but was depressed and very isolated. The more aggressively Maureen tried to get this family together, the more they resisted.

Maureen's own history had included hospitalization for severe depression several years ago after her divorce. She confided to me in a separate session that she was very frightened that this might happen again. The coping mechanism that she'd used in the past included a great deal of denial and attempts to control and "cheer everyone up." We discussed the fact that this was not working and that she needed to confront the family problems directly, while recognizing that she could not make changes for the other family members.

I suggested that we try something different for one session, namely, have Ray and the two boys attend, but without Maureen. At first Maureen was reluctant to agree to this. However, as we continued to discuss the fact that she dominated and tried to control what happened in the family, she eventually came to see that this was actually hurting communication among the others.

As it turned out, the session without Maureen was very successful. Ken, the 14-year-old, openly discussed the fact that ever since his father left he had felt that no one cared about him. His mother had a new husband, his older brother was always out doing things with friends, and he himself was left alone.

Tommy, who had taken over the father role for years, was supportive of his younger brother, but then turned angrily to his stepfather and said, "You know, we were doing fine without you. You don't even have a regular job. My mother makes more than you do. You just sponge off us and act like a lazy jerk."

"I act like a jerk?" countered Ray. "What about you? I can smell the grass in your bedroom. Maybe your mother doesn't know you're stoned half the time, but I do. Your best buddy Jim was arrested for dealing drugs last month, you're failing half of your courses and might not even graduate this year, and you criticize me?"

"Look," I said, "there's a lot of understandable anger and tension in this family. Up until now, Maureen has tried to keep everyone happy but has ended up in the middle without letting you guys deal with your own issues. I wanted to get you together to start looking at whatever is going on with the three of you."

Ken said that he really liked his stepfather Ray, and even worried about him because Ray seemed to have become more sullen and withdrawn after moving in six months ago when he married Maureen. Ray indicated some surprise and said that was funny because he thought the same about Ken—both that he really liked Ken and that he worried about him. Ken and Ray wanted and needed a relationship with each other, and they more or less needed permission and encouragement to have that without feeling it had to be approved by Maureen.

Tommy was dealing with his usurped paternal role by using drugs and misdirecting his anger. By talking with Ray, he realized that his stepfather was a decent, caring man who did not mean to interfere with Tommy's relationship with his mother or brother. It also became clear in the two sessions with the three of them that Tommy was developing a significant drug dependency. Furthermore, the boy's own social system had shifted dramatically in the past year. He was neglecting his former neighborhood friends, who were generally good students and active in school activities, and his current system included primarily drug abusers who had dropped out of school. His closest friend, Jimmy, had been arrested for selling cocaine, and Tommy broke down in tears as he talked of his fears that he was having a problem getting off it himself.

The three of them agreed to help each other and to talk more directly. It was also agreed that each had his own issues. Tommy was immediately referred to a drug abuse program, where it was decided that he needed to be hospitalized. Ken began individual counseling to deal with his depression, which was found to be relatively minor and very amenable to improvement through Ray's attention. Ray found that he could help the two boys as well as himself by caring for them and opening up himself. He continued in brief therapy with me.

Maureen was unburdened of the responsibility for keeping her new husband and her two boys content. I had multiple sessions with Maureen and Ray as a couple, and they discussed ways of communicating better without feeling responsible for the other partner's feelings. As the two boys improved in treatment and communication opened up more directly with each family member, the family system vastly improved. I continued in close contact with both of the boys' therapists, and we all met on two occasions to discuss progress and ways of keeping up the dialogue. The problem had been that all communication was directed to Maureen, who then accepted responsibility for everyone else's feelings. Furthermore, she inadvertently interfered with, rather than facilitated, communication. She needed to remove herself from the middle and let her husband and the boys work out their own relationships. The family tensions lifted rather quickly, as did some of the individual anger and depression. Tommy's problem with drugs, however, was significant, and when I closed with this family, the problem was still ongoing.

The case management approach was used in this instance because each family member needed to deal separately with his or her own issues. Furthermore, the family dynamics had been counterproductive in that all communication was channeled through Maureen, who then accepted responsibility for everyone else's well-being. She was inadvertently hurting communication, because her sons and her new husband actually needed to work out some of the issues among and between themselves. By putting herself in the middle, Maureen kept them apart. The case management approach both allowed for family sessions and supported the need to deal with individual issues.

NASW's "Family Support Principles"

NASW has developed a consultation network to promote a better understanding of the family. NASW's Commission on Families has defined *family* as "two or more people who consider themselves 'family' and who assume obligations, functions and responsibilities generally essential to healthy family life" (National Association of Social Workers, Commission on Families, 1989 unpublished). This broad definition encompasses diverse family structures, life cycles, and cultural influences. Thus, a family could include a single mother living with her child, or three elderly men, or a single woman and her foster child.

NASW and its Commission on Families has further stated that families may need outside support to maintain healthy functioning. This support can come from the formal social services system; from the informal system of family, friends, and neighbors; or from some collaboration of the two, as recommended by the social support system approach presented in this book. Following is the complete text of *Family Support Principles* as recommended by NASW for working with families.

Family Support Principles

- Family support programs should be preventive in nature whenever possible. However, such principles may also apply to services to high-risk families.
- Family support services should be family and community based.
- Presenting problems should be defined in terms of family and community systems.
- Case plans should be based on families' definition of problems, goals, needs, and solutions. Whenever possible, case plans should be based on families' strengths, not deficits.
- Service planning should be designed to enhance choices offered to families. A variety of program options could include home health services, respite care, family support groups, and in-home care as opposed to nursing home care. Resource/program development activities should be undertaken to assure the availability of service options.
- Problems and solutions should be defined in terms of families/ culture, ethnicity, and heritage.

- Services must be tailored to fit families rather than forcing families to fit into categorical services.
- Service philosophy should reflect a "no reject" approach to families.
- Services must be accessible.
- Services must reflect skill acquisition and resource mobilization in addition to addressing clients' cognitive, behavioral, and emotional problems.
- Services must address not only symptoms but conditions that cause them.
- Family support strategies must reflect a multi-modal approach and be framed within an advocacy approach to the family.
- Service delivery systems must be family-friendly (e.g., family interviewing rooms).
- Management practice and policy must reflect family-supportive values and approaches.
- Management practices and policies must be responsive to cultural diversity.
- Social workers and administrators must demonstrate attempts to link innovative family support services to systemwide policy and service reform.
- Social workers should replicate tested models of family support innovations.
- Family support innovations should be designed as empirically testable demonstration projects.
- Development of services should reflect the appropriate roles for the life-cycle stages of individuals.

Questions

1. An ongoing dilemma for social work practitioners concerns the issue of using marginally functional families in the therapeutic process. What general issues do you consider in deciding whether to include or exclude a family that has targeted your client as the scapegoat or the "problem of the family"?

2. The norm for the composition of the American family is no longer simply a married mother and father with their biological children. In your practice experience, what are the

most common compositions of the families you see? Try to list four types, in the order of frequency, seen in your agency or practice.

3. What specific cultural, racial, or ethnic considerations must you use in working with the families in your practice? How do you incorporate these into social support systems development?

4. Discuss the merits of case management, network intervention, and general system development when working with entire family systems. In answering this question, you may want to refer back to chapter 2 as well as consider this chapter's content.

References

Campbell, A., Converse, P. E., & Rodgers, W. L. (1976). *The quality of American life: Perspective, evaluations and satisfaction.* New York: Russell Sage Foundation.

Caplan, G. (1974). *Support systems and community mental health.* New York: Behavioral Publications.

Christensen, H. T. (1968). Children in the family: Relationships of number and spacing to marital success. *Journal of Marriage and the Family, 30,* 283–289.

England, P., & Farkas, G. (1986). *Households, employment and gender: A social, economic and demographic view.* New York: Aldine.

Hobbs, P. F., & Cole, S. P. (1976). Transition to parenthood: A decade of replication. *Journal of Marriage and the Family, 38,* 723–731.

Hoffman, L.W., & Manis, J.D. (1978). Influences of children on marital interaction and parental satisfactions and dissatisfactions. In R.M. Lerner & G. B. Spanier (Eds.). *Child influences on marital and family interaction: A life span perspective.* New York: Academic Press.

Lepman, A., & Longino, C. F. (1982). Formal and informal support: A conceptual clarification. *Journal of Applied Gerontology , 1,* 141–146.

Levitan, S., & Belous, R. S. (1981). *What's happening to the American family?* Baltimore, MD: Johns Hopkins University Press.

Maguire, L., & Martz, P. (in press). Youth face unemployment: An international comparison. In J. C. Cunningham and P. Martz (Eds.), *Family matters.* Pittsburgh: University of Pittsburgh Press.

McGoldrick, M., Pearce, J. K., & Giordano, J. (Eds.). (1982). *Ethnicity and family therapy.* New York: Guilford Press.

National Association of Social Workers, Commission on Families. (1989). *Promoting family supports.* Silver Spring, MD: Author.

Rollins, B. C., & Gelligan, R. (1978). The developing child and marital satisfaction of parents. In R. M. Lerner & G. B. Spanier (Eds.), *Child influences on marital and family interaction: A life span perspective.* New York: Academic Press.

Spiegel, J. (1982). An ecological model of ethnic families. In M. McGoldrick, J. K. Pearce, & J. Giordano (Eds.), *Ethnicity and family therapy* (pp. 31–54). New York: Guilford Press.

Chapter 6

Social Support Systems in the Life Stages

Childhood

Childhood development begins at conception. The genes of the parents mingle to form an embryo that inherits certain characteristics from the parents. Among these are physical traits (blue eyes, black hair, a lean frame, large feet) and others, such as an ability to perceive and to re-create images well, thus enabling a person to be an artist if the traits are developed. Similarly, one may be born with a capacity to organize symbols well and to think deductively, thus having the potential to do well in mathematics or science if those traits are developed.

Social abilities are also partially a result of inherited traits and learned behaviors. The Freudians perceive young infants as being orally oriented, receiving nurturance and gratification through sucking and eating. If this stage is generally accomplished satisfactorily (that is, if the infant is not overly frustrated), he or she can go on to the next developmental stage, the anal stage. If not nurtured or nurtured only erratically or hostilely, however, the infant could become fixated at the oral stage, eventually developing, for instance, an eating disorder or habits of excessive drinking, smoking, or talking.

At the anal stage, during which the toddler first learns to control his or her bodily functions, the child develops personality traits that relate to being more giving or retentive, more controlling of oneself and others or more trusting and flexible in social exchanges.

From a social support system perspective, the early developmental stages described by Erik Erickson seem even more relevant. He views the earliest stage as being focused on either trust or mistrust. The young infant learns from its mother in most instances whether he or she will be fed, cleaned, and cared for. If the infant has its basic nurturant needs met in a loving manner, he or she learns to trust the world as being giving and caring. The infant in a loving situation is basically being assured of survival and growth, and the child can then develop in the knowledge that others care for and will protect him or her. Without such basic needs being adequately met, however, the young infant learns that it cannot trust the world or its environment to satisfy its needs. In extreme cases of neglect infants may die. More often, they survive physically but they mistrust others, having learned that they cannot rely on others and that they must take care of themselves.

According to Erickson, toddlers are learning autonomy versus shame and doubt. They are learning to be autonomous and will be more confident when they are allowed and encouraged to explore their environment and come to know that they are separate, capable beings who can master the world around them and who will be rewarded for learning. They have been supported by their parents or by others who let them know that their behavior and feelings and actions evoke a response in others and that their world is composed of people who care and will respond to them in a giving manner. However, if the social system punishes or ignores toddlers when interacting with others, they learn to be ashamed or doubtful about themselves and their environment. The developing toddler's response to such an unwelcoming environment is likely to be that social isolation is preferable to dependency on something that makes one feel frightened, ashamed, and insecure. In some instances the developing response is to become a clinging, needy person who believes deep inside that no matter how hard he or she tries, others will be disappointed.

A third perspective on early childhood development is that of Jean Piaget, who has described it in terms of four discrete and qualitatively different stages: (1) the sensorimotor period, which takes place during infancy; (2) the preoperational period, from about two to seven years of age; (3) the stage of concrete operations, from age seven to 11; and (4) the formal operations stage, which begins usually after the age of 12.

This cognitive approach to development is a rather biological model which suggests that individuals develop schemes to process information. These schemes change and become more complete as the child matures and learns through interaction and development. Very young children are observed to be egocentric and even assume that everyone else views the world the same way they do. They are also very concrete in their thinking and limited in their perceptions. As they grow and develop, these schemes allow them to take more into account, such as social skills. Their cognitive skills are enhanced through social interactions that allow them to develop skills such as talking, moving, watching, verbalizing, and manipulating their environment. Through social situations, developing youngsters learn to interact in a way that lets them learn how to achieve their goals. Parents and teachers need to allow youngsters to be exposed to social systems that encourage the learning of new social skills must and interactional capabilities. Such developmental skills must be paced and manageable for the child, and suitable for their cognitive ability. For instance, a two-year-old who wants a certain toy will simply take it away from another child. Knowing or caring that the other two-year-old will respond negatively to this action, or even knowing that the other child exists as a separate entity, is simply not possible at this age. But by five, the child knows better, and realizes that there are social consequences to such behavior as well.

Although the cognitive theories explain intellectual development and reasoning better than the theories of the psychoanalysts or Ericksonians, their ability to explain psychosocial or sexual development or even such issues as dependence, or aggression or hostility, are more limited. According to cognitive theories, social support system development is a process of learning first to differentiate self from the environment and then of developing concrete thinking into more socially and interactionally appropriate processes (Specht & Craig, 1987).

The common theme among these various theories of child development is that children need to have basic needs met in a caring and supportive manner in order to learn how to trust and to become autonomous, but caring, individuals. If infants are given affection and nurturance consistently, they learn that it is safe to trust, grow, explore, learn, interact, and manipulate. They learn that they are acceptable to others and that they can affect their environment, that the social system cares and responds to them in a reasonable and somewhat consistent manner, and that if they give to others, others will generally return the giving (Lerner & Lerner, 1986).

Preschool children at the ages of four, five, and six have learned these rudimentary social skills, although in an immature way. They are still testing and learning and are limited in terms of both cognitive and psychosocial ability. At this age, however, personalities that point to lifelong patterns of behavior are clearly emerging. General tendencies toward aggressiveness or passivity, caring or distrust have been formed. The basics of the personality are believed by the Freudians to be formed at the age of six.

The effectiveness or lack of parenting skills and the influence of cultural practices become more self-evident as preschoolers develop. The verbal exchanges and other interactions of parents and children form the basis for children's future patterns of interaction. The parent who discusses issues and instructs without demanding conformity or strict adherence to authority lays the foundation for an adult who can make decisions with confidence. At the extremes in child raising, too much of a laissez-faire attitude may have consequences as negative as those resulting from a domineering, authoritarian manner. Young children need to be protected and guided but not threatened or coerced into certain behaviors.

Children model their parents' behavior and learn how to develop social support systems and relationships by imitating or reacting to parental behavior. Parents who are actively engaged with other adults in appropriate community, social, cultural, or religious activities model the same healthy interactions for their children. Similarly, parents who are isolated from others or who distrust family and neighbors and withdraw socially in the face of stress or adversity are modeling similar behavior. Although parental example is only one of many determinants of social behavior, it is a strong one. Others include parenting skills, cultural orientation, and structural socioeconomic forces such as neighborhood, school, and church. Identification with one parent, usually the parent of the same sex as the child, also shapes values, attitudes, and social skills (Kreppner & Lerner, 1989).

The social life of children is different from that of adults. Children enter the world entirely reliant on their parents or on others not only to keep them alive but to nurture them and help them develop a sense of self. The family provides the entree to the socialization process, and the way the child interacts with parents, siblings, and others in those first few crucial years and months establishes lifelong patterns (Lerner & Lerner, 1986).

Despite the influence of family, however, social workers also frequently marvel at the resiliency and strength of youngsters who apparently transcend their adverse social systems and do well in spite of them. The caseload of social workers who work with children almost invariably includes many examples of abused children who protect their parents, neglected children who nurture their parents, and children of alcoholic or drug-addicted parents who display a seeming level of maturity and responsibility for others that goes far beyond what one would expect. In all such instances, unfortunately, these problems come back in later life to haunt the child as an adult.

Although some young children display an amazing ability to adapt and to grow even within dysfunctional family social systems, extreme cases of abuse or neglect can cause their death. Milder forms and variations of abuse are more frequent. The problem for the social worker is that the child is brought in to be treated and yet the child can more appropriately be seen as the result or symptom of the family social system's dysfunction. The child cannot be successfully treated unless the system that originated and maintains the need for the child's behavior is altered. The younger the child, the greater the need to focus on the system. As the child gets older, particularly when he or she is in the midteen to late teen years, the need to focus on the dysfunctional family system diminishes. At least in terms of the child's needs, he or she can become less reliant on the dysfunctional family system and may even be encouraged to separate from it, emotionally if not physically, as soon as possible.

Jimmy's Need for Attention

Jimmy was a seven-year-old boy, strikingly good looking, charming, and of above-average intelligence. He was the middle child in a family of three children. His older sister was "the good one," with excellent grades and good friends—a child who was "no trouble." The youngest girl was five, had been diagnosed as possibly autistic, and had been in and out of two institutions already. The parents frequently said that the emotional and financial strain related to her was more than either of them could bear.

Jimmy himself was manipulative, had an attention-deficit disorder and a history of violent outbursts, and used denial and avoidance extensively. His parents, Joe and Ellen, initially appeared to be models of hardworking but overwhelmed individuals with limited emotional, financial, and intellectual resources. They both worked two jobs, both had left high school before completing it, and both indicated that they were exhausted and becoming increasingly disgusted with Jimmy.

After a few sessions with the three of them, it became apparent that Ellen was severely depressed and resentful of her alcoholic, detached, and seemingly unsupportive husband. In a separate session, she said that she would leave Joe, but she had no place to go, especially with three children, two of whom were quite disturbed.

Joe's response to the family problems was to work night and day at two low-paying jobs both to make money and to avoid his depressed wife and disturbed children.

The first two sessions with the three of them went poorly. Ellen's anger and depression were such that she tearfully vented her rage at a seemingly passive husband, who occasionally looked at me and said, "She's crazy. I don't know why I put up with this." I had Jimmy leave for part of the sessions, because he was largely being ignored by both parents, and his mother's language and behavior were abusive. Unfortunately, she needed and used these opportunities as her only chance to tell Joe how angry she was at him and how depressed she was that she received no emotional support or affection from him. These issues had to be addressed, but Joe made it clear that he did not want to discuss them and that he would not return to the sessions— or possibly even to his family—if she continued berating him.

It was at this point that I began separate sessions with Ellen. I encouraged her to ventilate a great deal of anger and rage, much of which became directed at me as a male. In fact, various attempts of mine to see the family problems in a more balanced perspective were angrily countered by accusations that I was taking her husband's side and that, as a man, I could never understand what she was feeling. I asked her to help me understand these problems better, and I assured her that I would try to help her and that indeed she had suffered enormously.

I also helped her realize that she and her husband seemed to be so overwhelmed and hurt that they were hindering rather than helping each other. We also discussed her current dilemma: as she correctly assessed the situation, she had to ventilate her feelings and express them to Joe, knowing that the more expressively she did this the more withdrawn and avoidant he would become. We therefore decided to continue joint sessions, but she would work with me to get Joe to open up rather than to withdraw.

We also had one session with Ellen's mother and sister, both of whom were extremely supportive of her. In that session, both her mother and her sister spoke of the cruelty of Ellen's father, who had abandoned the family when Ellen was eight years old. Ellen had apparently been the only family member to occasionally stand up to him. We discussed the fact that while Joe was far from perfect, he was concerned about the children and loved them. We also discussed the fact that although her rage and disappointment were understandable, directing them all at her passive husband was counterproductive at the present time.

Ellen was referred to a women's support group at a local YWCA. After some hesitation and a few missed sessions, she eventually became involved with the group, which turned out to be particularly helpful to her not only because it allowed and encouraged her to express her feelings, but because it let her know that such feelings are understandable and are shared by others. Ellen was also referred to a feminist therapist who validated her feelings while helping her get personal control over her own life. Their discussions included examining the advantages and disadvantages of her marriage to Joe.

Joe was tremendously relieved by his wife getting help. In a series of separate sessions with me, he managed to open up enough to admit that he was frightened by both the severity of the disturbance in two of his children and by his wife's rage and hurt. At first both Joe and his wife blamed Joe and his lack of caring or action. However, Joe said he simply felt helpless and "weak," and that the more his wife berated him for his inadequacy, the more hurt, angry, and withdrawn he became. Although he was not particularly insightful, he became significantly more supportive of his wife and children when the pressure on him diminished and he began to talk.

Jimmy's attention deficit decreased when the family became more stable. He was put on medication and carefully monitored at home and at school. He was referred to a day program in a local psychiatric hospital for youngsters with attention deficits; the program was primarily behavioral in orientation. He also began playing in a local neighborhood soccer league through which he began developing friendships. His confidence grew considerably as he recognized that he could channel and control his energy, and that when he did so successfully other children liked him. Although some parents of neighborhood children continued for quite some time to keep their children from playing with Jimmy, he generally became more accepted even by those families.

Adolescence

In adolescence, children continue to grow and mature in the socialization process. In fact, the pressure to conform in order to be accepted is particularly apparent at this stage. The young person who does not dress and think in a manner acceptable to a clique or peer group runs the risk of being ostracized. Social ostracism is a particularly cruel form of rejection that is practiced among adolescents. It has grave consequences. Suicide attempts and major bouts with reactive depression are frequently preceded by rejection by highly demanding social cliques or boyfriends or girlfriends (Lerner & Galambos, 1984).

The social support systems of adolescents are primitive forms of the social systems of adults and serve as indicators of the sociability of these future adults. Adults simply practice social ostracism more subtly. An adolescent whose clothes are not in style with the dictates of his or her clique risks ridicule, a punishment that is rather severe for the relatively fragile ego of one already dealing with issues of sexuality, maturation, and oncoming adult responsibility.

Patterns of response are somewhat firmly established at this age, and by the end of adolescence, lifelong trends are observable. For instance, unless he or she receives help, the teenager who withdraws and isolates when criticized by friends at school will likely do the same as an adult when criticized at work or in the community. It is particularly useful to intervene in the social support system of adolescents at this stage, when patterns are still developing and when sensitivity to such issues is particularly high.

The social systems of adolescents are far from uniform. Early adolescence, at age 12 or 13, differs considerably from the late-adolescent attitudes and behaviors of 17-year-olds. In recent observations of members of a Girl Scout troop, ages 12 to 15, this author heard topics of discussion ranging from Teddy bears and doll collections to the relative sex appeal of various rock singers. These girls also practiced rather strict segregation by age (or grade) and followed a rather rigid pecking order of authority. The older girls associated with each other, and the younger girls formed a separate clique even within the troop. Close friendships existing outside of the troop (for instance between some 13- and 14-year-olds in different grades) were usually suspended during troop activities.

Status and prestige within the social system of adolescents are often based on personality characteristics such as confidence or forcefulness and leadership qualities. They are secondarily based on characteristics that, even though more superficial, are valued by the peer group—for example physical appearance, intelligence or grades in school, dress, athletic ability, or wealth.

The social systems of adolescent boys are similar to but even more primitive socially than those of girls, although this does not signify a lack of complexity in certain ways. Boys are verbally and socially less developed than girls in adolescence. The peer group is tremendously important, but some of the criteria with regard to boys' acceptance and status differ from those for girls. For instance, a high school senior who is an excellent football player is given a great deal of status, at least by most of the mainstream cliques, regardless of his social skills.

Gender issues are particularly salient for adolescents, and a factor in those, again, is the issue of conformity to certain norms. The young man who appears or acts effeminate or who has already accepted a homosexual orientation will often be rejected by the mainstream or "popular" cliques. His options are to join or develop an alternative social support system or to withdraw. The need for social support system intervention at the age of adolescence is apparent with such youngsters. At that stage, when conformity is essential to acceptance and the needs and insecurities are great, stress is potentially very high. Possessing only rudimentary and often superficial or stereotypical understanding of human differences, adolescents are trying to under-stand themselves and their place in society. Under such conditions, rigid rules of behavior and even of appearance are occasionally developed, or at least perceived, by insecure teenagers.

Just as with adults, acceptability and status for children vary a great deal depending on culture, gender, education, income, religion, and innumerable other variables that are defined by one's peer group. If the developing child has come through the previous life stages with a flexible and accepting attitude toward himself or herself and others and has a relatively high level of self-esteem and confidence, then the vicissitudes of acceptance and rejection by various peers are manageable.

Jenny the Perfect Teen

Jenny was a 16-year-old junior in high school who was brought in by her mother several weeks after her hospitalization. She had been in the hospital for several days following a sexual experience with a boy from school. Apparently she had been a virgin and not only lost her virginity but was sufficiently bruised and frightened to have sought medical care, which she very reluctantly had to receive with her mother's assistance.

She and her mother had gone to Jenny's pediatrician, who was alarmed enough to put her in the hospital under the care of a gynecologist. At first Jenny would not say what had happened or with whom she'd had intercourse. The mother found out this information from Jenny's friends and planned to have the boy charged with rape and assault. Even after Jenny tearfully explained to her irate and disbelieving mother that the boy had neither assaulted nor raped her, the mother still wanted to press charges.

Jenny was a cheerleader, an honors student, a class officer, and her mother's ideal. She had rigidly conformed herself to satisfy her mother's desire for a popular and beautiful daughter. In fact, she had rigidly conformed to all of her mother's requirements. Up until a few weeks before the session, she had been, at least on the surface, the perfect teen.

The reality was that Jenny had passively accepted her mother's dominating authority but had rebelled by becoming involved with a boy who was totally unacceptable to her family or even to Jenny's status-conscious clique at high school. In fact, the mother had not brought Jenny in because of depression or the trauma of the first, painful sexual experience. She brought her in because Jenny for the first time in her life was angrily confronting her mother and had been calling the boy even from her hospital bed.

At the first session, the social worker noted the fact that the mother and daughter were both very fashionably dressed, were both precisely and similarly coiffed, and were both very attractive blue-eyed blondes. However, a look of quiet despair was apparent on Jenny's face as her mother began by explaining that some "horrible boy used Jenny" and now Jenny believed she was in love with him. The mother then quickly and emphatically described how Jenny had always been the perfect child—how she had had excellent grades, associated with the youngsters that her parents chose, was popular, and until a few weeks ago, had always strictly obeyed her parents.

The social worker then spoke alone with Jenny, who almost immediately began to cry. Her distress, however, was caused by the fact that the boy she loved did not call her back. She explained that her father had called the boy's parents and accused him of assault and rape but said that if their son stayed away from his daughter, he would not press charges.

The problems in this family were many, and the family members had different goals. Jenny's parents were unable to deal with their daughter's developing sexuality or her rebellion. They wanted her to return to being their "pure," bright, popular cheerleader daughter whose life, up until this time, had been everything the mother wanted for herself. The parents preferred to believe that the boy had forced himself on their daughter, when in fact Jenny had pursued him. The boy was also a 16-year-old junior and a classmate in several honors classes with Jenny. However, he was considered to be a "loner" and did not associate with any of the popular cliques of Jenny and her friends.

The ventilation stage for mother, daughter, and father was extremely difficult. This was a family that valued appearances and "doing the right thing." Conformity and acceptance were extremely important, and what had begun as covert rebellion and sexual curiosity on Jenny's part had become a very open, public, traumatic, and embarrassing event for everyone.

Jenny swore that she would not return to school, because "everyone knew," and she believed that her reputation had swiftly gone from the girl "most likely to be senior prom queen to the class slut" overnight. The social worker encouraged the family to discuss these fears very openly before assessing them. A related fear that needed to be discussed was that if Jenny did not return to school, or even if her grades dropped dramatically, she would not go to a good college. Both of the parents lived vicariously through their daughter's successes, and neither of them had attended college. Jenny's academic success in high school and assumed success in college was now threatened for these parents, who had come to see college as an opportunity for upward mobility for their daughter.

The assessment involved looking realistically at the facts and related feelings. Discussions ensued about the most likely reaction of family, friends, and neighbors. It gradually became apparent that although some of Jenny's adolescent friends who were particularly superficial would probably distance themselves from her, her real friends would not.

For purposes of clarification the social worker had Jenny draw two versions of her social network diagram. The first was to represent her social network as it had been in the weeks before she spent the evening with the boy, and the second, her current network, four weeks after the fateful evening. The social worker had already been careful to get Jenny and her parents to examine their feelings and the facts realistically and emotionally. The two diagrams were somewhat realistic in that they reflected the superficiality of some of Jenny's previous friendships, which were based on adolescent standards of popularity. The second network diagram reflected a strong core of good, faithful friends, specifically, two girls who had been Jenny's genuinely close friends and confidants for many years. In fact, one of them was not a part of the popular clique of most of Jenny's friends.

Clarification also focused on the circumstances that had led to Jenny's secretly taking a lover who was unacceptable to both her clique and her parents. The social worker helped them all discuss the normal, healthy sexual instincts of teenagers as well as their need to become separate and autonomous. They eventually came to see that the pressure of constantly conforming to her mother's desires and the demands of her clique had become overwhelming for Jenny. This "perfect teen" could no longer tolerate the pressure, and when she found a nice boy who was nearly everything disapproved of by both her clique and her parents, she pursued him. The evening she spent with him had apparently been excessive physically and emotionally, and it had frightened Jenny. It also awakened a great flood of pent-up feelings that Jenny had denied to her parents and even herself. These issues were discussed at length in separate sessions with the social worker, who encouraged Jenny to recognize and deal with her feelings.

The planning stage centered around rebuilding a strong social support system composed of genuine and loyal friends. This was also a useful learning experience for mother and daughter, because it became apparent that several of the so-called friends the mother had advanced were the first to abandon Jenny. One, for instance, was a very popular young girl, known to be manipulative, who was among the first to turn on Jenny. By contrast, several good childhood friends whom Jenny had ignored recently were there to help her. Jenny and her mother were forced to reevaluate their values and plan accordingly.

The restructuring of the system involved significant shifts. The cheerleaders, with one exception, avoided Jenny, because many rumors in school had apparently circulated. Jenny herself needed to be convinced that her best strategy was to assert herself without forcing herself on anyone. She knew that she had not changed and was still the same decent young woman she had always been. Now she was wiser and had learned a great deal about herself and about the nature of real friendships and concern. The boys and girls she'd befriended and who in turn came to her support were sincere, genuine, loyal people who cared for her because of herself. Those who had abandoned her were for the most part superficial friends or people who felt some malice, hostility, or jealousy toward her.

The relationship with the boy did not succeed. Its failure, however, was because of Jenny's realization that much of the attraction had grown out of a desire to rebel covertly and out of sexual curiosity and repression. She did not begin dating again for some time, but the social worker helped her to work through and better understand issues of sex, love, infatuation, and genuine caring and friendships. She looked forward to college and to a new beginning as a maturing young woman with a better sense of who she was and what her values were socially and personally.

In the case of Jenny, several strongly held viewpoints were confronted. The parents were reluctantly forced to see that many of their priorities and values were superficial. Physical and social appearances had taken precedence over genuine decency and friendships. Furthermore, Jenny needed to assert herself independently and stop being the object of her parents' unfulfilled hopes. As traumatic as this experience was to that family, it was also a tremendously positive factor in getting all of them to reexamine their feelings toward each other and toward themselves as individuals. Crisis led to change and, in this case, change led to growth and self-knowledge. The intervention of a social worker at such times can be a powerful tool in directing the change in a positive way for the individuals involved, the family, and the larger social support system.

Adulthood

Adulthood encompasses many separate stages. There are tremendous differences between a person in his or her early 20s and the same person in the late 50s. The career of the young adult is just beginning or still being chosen, whereas that of the older adult is winding down, and retirement plans are often under serious consideration. The young adult is often single and just starting to look for a lifelong partner; the older adult is often in a long-term relationship and beginning to lose children to marriages and careers of their own. Between these two stages, adults go through numerous phases related to beginning families and careers, dealing with existential or midlife crises, redefining relationships with their aging parents, and other issues.

This author has run dozens of workshops over the years related to analyzing social support systems. In these workshops I have always asked participants to draw their social network diagrams. From these diagrams certain consistent findings have become apparent for most adults. For instance, it appears that in early adulthood, roughly age 20 through 28, individuals are developing the two areas for which they had prepared for most of their lives: family and career. Males and females alike are still expected, if not pressured, by family and friends to "settle down," get married, and begin raising a family. Some, of course, begin families while still in their teens, others not until later, and many choose not to marry or raise families. But the norm is still to marry in early adulthood and begin raising a family (Levinson, 1978).

Observations of participants in workshops indicated that the social support system of young adults varies depending on gender and marital status. Females more often have close female friends, and males also prefer close female friends because they are often more comfortable confiding in women than in other males. This phenomenon exists throughout life: married women often indicate that other women, not their husbands, are still their closest friends and confidants. For a married man the person often valued as best friend and confidant is his wife.

The social support systems of young adults often change with marriage. Whereas young adult males and females often socialize in same-gender groups, the social system becomes couple-oriented with marriage. Typically, young married couples begin to gravitate toward other young married couples with similar interests and backgrounds. Social life begins to center more around dinners and home visits than around bars frequented by single people. Social support systems tend to find commonality, and in the case of young married couples these systems further require the abandonment of previous life-styles.

Young married couples actively discourage their partners from maintaining too many ties with old friends who are still single. In short, young married women rarely support their spouses' continued involvement with single friends—especially females—and men are extremely unlikely to support their wives' continuing interaction with single men friends. While same-sex friendships are common and can remain very close, especially among women, the activities change.

In workshops that I have run in the homosexual community, many variations of social systems are apparent, with a pronounced shift in the last decade toward more ongoing, monogamous relationships. Again, some gender differences exist in that lesbians have long been more couple-oriented, whereas among male homosexuals relationships are monogamous more often than in the past, partly because of the fear of AIDS and other sexually transmitted diseases. This change has had several positive effects in that it has encouraged strong, ongoing, familial types of bonds. The depth, consistency, and intimacy inherent in such ongoing social support systems have been viewed by many in the homosexual community as being a tremendous force in helping them combat the bias and social prejudice that are still so strong in society against them.

When some young married couples have children, their social support system again undergoes changes. Over the past 10 years, I have had my students studying for their Master of Social Work (MSW) degree draw their social network diagrams and discuss them and their changes. The majority of these students are in their middle to late 20s or early 30s. In fact, because I do this four times a year with classes of 20 or more students, a total of about 800 social work students have been involved in this exercise.

It is useful for social workers to be required to examine their own social support systems. What I have found is that we too generally associate with people of similar ages, races, backgrounds, and interests. Furthermore, it often happens that social work students who as teenagers rebelled against the middle-class standards of their parents or others not too many years later find themselves involved in the same activities to which they had once objected. The single male or female working or attending school has a very different social system from that of the same person six years later with a young child. The latter is often very interested in issues related to toilet training, bonding, teething, and related concerns that were laughably remote a few short years earlier.

Network diagramming to analyze social support systems has been very helpful for these social work students because of the unrelenting clarity and objectivity of the information that it reveals. It makes them realize that social workers too are often less socially accepting of others than they would like to believe. The majority of the white students have white friends, and the majority of black students have primarily black friends. Young students generally have young friends, and older students older friends. Religion and ethnicity are also clear variables in the selection process even of the social networks of social workers.

Discussions of the homogeneity of social support systems with MSW students are often enlightening and interesting. The tendency to befriend others who are similar to oneself is neither good nor bad; it is simply normal. Even social workers should be allowed to surround themselves with family and friends who share their interests, backgrounds, and other characteristics. Problems develop only when they become too narrow in their viewpoints, which is likely when all of one's associates share the same point of view. A person's values and actions are reinforced by friends, and although such systems do provide support, they can also lead one to be more myopic in his or her point of view.

The social lives of single parents, the vast majority of whom are female, are particularly stressful and difficult. Recent research (Yamatani, Maguire, Rogers, & O'Kennedy, in press) indicates that the rates of depression are more than twice as high for single, unemployed adult females as for men (21.3 percent for single females versus 9.2 percent for single males). Part of the explanation is the economic disparity between the genders. In the random population in poor communities surrounding Pittsburgh that was the subject of this study, the rate of unemployment was 31.3 percent for single females and 17.2 percent for single males. Furthermore, single female heads of households had 24 percent less revenue than households headed by single males, which amounts to a total of $117 less per week for the households headed by females. The majority of the households headed by single females have children, but few of the male households do.

Patterns become apparent in the social systems of single people in early or even somewhat later adulthood. Children are provided for primarily by females, who have significantly higher unemployment rates because of the need for child care. Furthermore, studies indicate that even when the adults with the children are employed men, they make significantly more money than females (National Commission on Working Women, 1988). In the Yamatani et al. (in press) study, married people, male and female, made more money than single individuals ($31,400 for the employed and $16,600 for unemployed heads of households). Single males made $25,500 if employed and $11,100 if unemployed. Single females made $19,400 if employed and $8,800 if unemployed. At least in this study, the higher rates of depression in women appear to be related to practical, overwhelming economic and employment-related factors rather than to any particular predisposition toward depression based on gender. The women are simply required to raise more children on significantly less money than are their single male counterparts.

Divorce is another major experience and a life crisis encountered by roughly half of the adult American population. Observations of several hundred of my workshop participants over the years bear out the dramatic changes in social systems that accompany divorce, as discussed in chapter 5. The friends of couples must choose between the two former spouses or lovers. In some instances—for example, where close friendships with one partner predated the marriage—the choice is easy and obvious. However, the support systems in these instances are further complicated by the issue of social imbalance. Middle adulthood (generally, during one's 30s and 40s) often consists socially of couple-related or extended-family activities. With a divorce, the extended families often, but not always, part along kinship lines. Because the developed social support system of many adult couples is made up primarily of other adult couples, the divorce, or "de-coupling," leads to unattached males and females. It may not be particularly difficult for young adults who had brief marriages to reconnect with their old system of single friends, but it is very difficult for older, more established adults to do so. The trauma of a divorce can be quite devastating for men or women who have been married for 10, 20, or more years; established the traditional social system of similar, like-minded couples; and then found themselves alone. Not only is the loss of their social support system likely, but that problem is compounded by the difficulty in reestablishing a new one, particularly when the divorce itself tends to be so traumatic and psychologically devastating (Sprenkle, 1985).

For the man or woman who leaves the partner to pursue another, the results of divorce are less negative. Those who leave negatively stressful marriages can certainly benefit themselves. However, for the person abandoned or rejected and "clinging," the results are significant (Sprenkle, 1985). Not only does the abandoned party, male or female, generally feel alone and rejected, but that party often blames himself or herself for the abandonment and, as a consequence, his or her confidence and potential for rebuilding new social support systems are often impaired. They wonder why if their spouse did not care for them anyone else should. Because the couples-related network is often intolerant of sexual imbalance or threatened by "extra," unattached males or females in their closed system, the recently divorced individual rarely finds comfort in that same system (Weiss, 1975).

New social support systems composed of people whose partnerships have also ended are often the answer, particularly when combined with an approach that encourages "letting go" and recognizes the cognitive as well as the emotional results of divorce (Sprenkle, 1988). To begin forming new systems for themselves, divorced people sometimes join formal groups or organizations such as Parents Without Partners or church-related groups for divorced people and/or single parents. They often consciously or subconsciously find and begin relating to others who are divorced or to individuals with recently broken attachments. Some women and men call friends who have gone through divorce. Depending on individual circumstances, divorced people may start dating right away, but most seem to prefer a period of nonsexual support from good friends. The person who feels compelled to jump quickly into another relationship is a common exception to the usual pattern. This phenomenon, called the rebound effect, often has negative consequences (Fisher, 1981).

Social support systems in later adulthood are also occasionally affected by midlife or existential crises (Sheehy, 1976; Levinson, 1978), which revolve around the realization that life is more than half over and around the related reflections of mature, responsible people as to the meaning or purpose of it all. The death of a parent, a divorce, or a similar tragedy such as job loss or injury to a child often precedes these crises. Occasionally there is no clear precipitating incident—just a sudden or developing need to understand oneself and one's place and purpose. These later adult life crises at times result in the person's leaving a marriage or job of many years and often of justifying the action by convincing himself or herself that the partner or job were really not suitable anyway. Friends and relatives in the social support system have three general responses to such decisions: they may be supportive and listen, try to convince the person to maintain the status quo, or try to talk him or her out of the change. The first response is usually the most helpful coming from members of the social support system (Kitson & Raschke, 1981). That is, by helping the person think carefully about such major changes, the support system is also helping the individual at least be allowed to reconsider the changes or to make them in a constructive manner. Trying to convince someone in such a crisis to maintain the status quo may later lead to anger, resentment, or reactionary behavior, as do attempts to get the person to stop considering change.

Older, mature adults who come to social workers for help with midlife or existential crises usually want or need changes in their social support system. In divorce or rejection, the individual needs to be reconnected to a new system, often including some associates from the old system. If the crisis is more a matter of dealing with existential issues of the meaning and purpose of life, quiet discussion, contemplation, and reading are as useful as more social interactions. Books or discussion groups or organizations involved with religious, philosophical, or psychological concerns are often helpful, as are adult education courses. Talking with others who are going through similar crises provides different viewpoints to consider.

At age 40 many men and women have more or less achieved or not achieved what they set out to do. Many have attained some inner peace, often supported by family, friends, and career accomplishments. Others have not and are still seeking it, often with increasing anxiety that their goals will never be reached. Still others are merely questioning their goals and accomplishments (Sheehy, 1976; Levinson, 1978). This stage of pausing to consider their past, present, and future is disconcerting for some people. Social workers often see men and women in their 40s who look back and see missed opportunities and partially met goals. Some, but not all, are socially isolated, never having married or formed other close, intimate, ongoing attachments. (The five major reasons for this failure to form close attachments are described in chapter 3 as typically being related to faulty perceptions of one's social support systems, poor self-esteem, depression, partial or incomplete types of support, and poor social skills.)

The social worker can often help develop a social support system for such clients using the approach described in this volume. However, there are inherent limitations for some people, and reality demands that the barriers and problems of each individual client be considered. A 45-year-old man or woman with little previous success in developing relationships, for example, is not going to reverse this lifelong pattern significantly with a few sessions. The painfully shy, withdrawn, or socially inadequate middle-aged person is not helped by being pushed beyond his or her limits.

The Secretary

Sally was a 42-year-old single woman who had worked as a secretary since high school graduation. Other than being noticeably anxious, she presented initially as a very normal, healthy, "average" person. She had never been married, engaged, or sexually involved with anyone in her life. She had recently been "passed over" for a promotion at her company, having been told that she just did not seem to have supervisory capability. Despite Sally's 15 years of excellent work, a younger, more assertive secretary was given the promotion. This had happened a month before Sally came in, and she said that at first it had not bothered her, but recently she could not stop thinking about it, and this "slight" had caused her to question a great many aspects of her life.

"I really don't know why I came here. It's not like I'm crazy or even that upset, but I've been crying a lot lately, and I don't know—it seems so silly," she began.

The social worker assured her that whatever her feelings were, she could talk about them and that they probably had some very real meaning to her. Sally's ventilation continued as she explained that at age 42 she felt she had accomplished nothing and was now feeling very frightened and alone. She had no close friends or relatives, and even her mother, with whom she was not particularly close, was quite sick. Sally said that "everyone else has a family and friends" but that she was "a failure." She described herself as being very different from everyone else, a deviant who was unloved and unlovable, and she now feared that she would eventually die alone with no one even caring.

The social worker had Sally draw a network diagram. Sally had only her mother in the inner circle and an elderly aunt whom she had not seen or spoken with in three years on the outer part. The friends that she listed were two other secretaries at work, neither of whom she saw socially or spoke with outside the office. She listed a dentist and an optometrist in the "other" category, but these relationships were also extremely distant. Encouragement, prodding, and suggestions from the social worker yielded no results. Sally was identified as a social isolate with virtually no previous history of close attachments.

The social worker encouraged her to clarify her thoughts and feelings. How long had she felt this way? What precipitated it? Had she had friends in the past? Who were they? What were they like? What sort of people and activities had she enjoyed in the past?

All of these questions and more were discussed to help develop a plan toward involving her in a meaningful way with others. Sally indicated that she had always wanted to be married and raise a family and she still hoped to do this. The social worker therefore worked with her further exploring her feelings about men and dating, and then helped plan ways for Sally to meet men with similar interests.

The planning phase for such a client must be developed along successful incremental stages, with small, manageable, successive steps designed to build gradually upon each other. Behavioral approaches have used this technique successfully for many years. However, the social worker had difficulty with Sally. She often avoided, "forgot," or unsuccessfully attempted even small, seemingly easy tasks. For instance, she never attended the singles group that she herself had discovered at a local church, nor did she ever go out to lunch with the one secretary in her office who she felt would befriend her. The planning stage floundered for nearly three months before the social worker decided to reconsider the approach.

"Sally, for several months we have talked about and planned ways for you to begin meeting and interacting more comfortably with others. Most of these plans have been your own ideas, and they were very good ones. But we seem to have problems in really getting things going. Maybe this is not right for you," the social worker suggested one day.

Sally and the social worker had developed good rapport and trust, but both were frustrated with their efforts, and so Sally decided to go back and try to understand better why this social system was not succeeding. Sally revealed that as a child she had never really been close to her mother. Her father had never married her mother (Sally had originally concealed this from the social worker), and Sally's mother seemed to have resented her daughter's very existence from birth. Furthermore, her mother neglected Sally as a child, leaving her for days with neighbors or with her grandmother. Sally further disclosed that when she was one year old she had been hospitalized with pneumonia and had run a fever for several days before being taken to the hospital. Her grandmother had reluctantly revealed all of this to Sally a few years before, saying that it was a "disgrace" the way her own daughter had nearly let Sally die of neglect. When that had happened the child protection worker had intervened, and Sally's mother was told that if her daughter was ever again hospitalized in her malnourished and anemic condition, her parental rights would be terminated.

This new information about Sally's early childhood history helped the social worker understand not only that Sally had had no previous attachment to anyone, but that initial bonding of any depth had never developed with her mother. Furthermore, the high fever, neglect, and malnourishment may have added some degree of permanent but subtle damage.

The system development approach was therefore reworked at a slower pace and with different expectations. Sally was encouraged to assess what she genuinely wanted socially, not what society expected of most people. Her anxiety and depression were partially the result of her lack of achievement of social norms. She needed to allow herself to define objectively the importance of close, intimate relationships for her. She ultimately decided that she did need to be involved socially just to relax and to remain busy, but that for the present she felt no need to find a husband or an intimate partner. As she slowly became more comfortable with herself and others, she could still choose to become more intimate, but it was not required in order to fulfill her life or somehow justify her existence.

People in their 30s or early 40s often pause to reflect upon their lives. It is a time to reexamine the past, present, and future (Sheehy, 1976). Many look with disappointment at lost opportunities in their personal and professional lives. Some make conscious decisions to change their lives or at least to make a last, major effort to reach lifelong goals. Others examine past goals and expectations and decide that such goals were not realistic or they were not consistent with their current values. For instance, at age 35, men and women have a relatively clear picture of whether or not they have achieved their goals in terms of marriage, family, income, status, or security. This examination is a significant life crisis or passage for many and a time in which social work intervention is often needed to put the past, present, and future into some meaningful perspective.

The Elderly

The aged are as diverse a group as any other category and perhaps even more so. They range from the healthy, independent senior employees of corporations to that smaller minority of totally dependent people living in institutions. The support systems among older people are primarily informal—family and friends. In fact, very few resources are provided by formal social services agencies, and the vast majority of their help comes from family (Atchley, 1988). Furthermore, even though income and health services are funded by federal and state programs, family members still provide assistance in those areas. Of even more significance, family members provide help in dealing with bureaucracies, offer encouragement, and include the elderly in general socialization activities that can rarely be provided at the same quality by nonfamily members (Shanas, 1979). Formal bureaucratic systems are often adequately equipped to provide health care and economic aid, but family and friends are better able to provide the personal caring and intimacy lacking in the formal system. The latter are the most meaningful and significant relationships and supports for the aged even though specialized medical care and even social services may become increasingly significant as people enter the "very old" category, over age 75.

Most middle-aged and older people at least begin this phase of life as a couple. Retirement and completion of the responsibilities of providing care for their children are frequently very positive forces in life and marital satisfaction. The stress and strain of jobs and child raising often give way to a fulfilling phase of life, at least for healthy, economically comfortable couples in their 60s (Atchley, 1988).

The curvilinear satisfaction rate described in chapter 5 is an important factor in old age. The high satisfaction rate with young marriages declines to a low point through middle age and in the period where females are raising teenagers at home or while couples with job stress and high community demands are having difficulty. When children leave home and retirement begins for these healthy and independent couples, life is frequently very rewarding and the divorce rate is relatively low (Holahan, 1984).

Life becomes more difficult for many in their 70s as frail health and the death of spouses and friends diminish their social support systems. At ages 75 and over, two-thirds of women are widows, although nearly 70 percent of men have spouses living with them (U.S. Bureau of the Census, 1983). Thus, most older men can rely on spouses, whereas older women must usually rely on their children or on people other than spouses for support.

Another consideration of very practical importance associated with advanced age is the physical limits it places on potential social support. In order to develop and even maintain social relationships, one must be able to communicate and interact. Such basic prerequisites for social engagement are often diminished for the frail elderly, whose hearing, eyesight, and mobility may become increasingly limited. In the past, such physical impairments led to social isolation and subsequent depression and lethargy that were frequently perceived as signs of senility. Geriatric social workers and others now know that social isolation and its negative psychosocial consequences can be stopped. Hearing aids, glasses, walkers, or wheelchairs can be used to allow physically frail but intellectually and socially vibrant older adults to stay busy, active, and alert. Loss of hearing, eyesight, or mobility need not mean the loss of social support, because such conditions can be treated.

Poverty is also associated with many psychosocial problems among the aged. In 1983, more than 14 percent of the aged in the United States lived at or below the poverty level, with certain minority populations being particularly hurt: this group included 42 percent of older black women and 24 percent of aged Hispanic women in this country (U.S. Senate Special Committee on Aging, 1986).

Poverty, like poor hearing or eyesight, is a potential cause of diminished social support. From a practical viewpoint, it translates for many into an inability to pay for transportation to go visiting, to pay for phone calls, or to entertain family or friends at home. Related issues such as embarrassment about one's clothing or the condition of one's housing unfortunately further curtail the possibility of developing active social lives for the elderly who are poor.

When comparing the poor, the near-poor, and the nonpoor, Auslander and Litwin (1988) found that the poor had significantly smaller networks than the near-poor and the nonpoor on the measures of availability of network ties. The poor reported fewer close relatives and fewer close ties to people with whom they interacted monthly. The poor were also significantly less involved with any type of volunteer organization or any other kind of group. In formal measurements of network involvement and perceived satisfaction, this study consistently found that the poor were less involved with any type of network. The perceived satisfaction with such ties was also lower for the poor than for either the near-poor or the nonpoor.

The aging client is affected by a wide range of factors, among them physical health and economic conditions, two factors that have a tremendous effect on the availability of social support systems and psychosocial health. Some elderly people who are very poor or in very poor health can maintain social support systems, but it is often difficult. Both conditions are, however, alterable, and it is those conditions that social workers need to address directly with the elderly. Even when the social worker has limited resources to provide, small amounts of assistance in these areas can have dramatic effects. For instance, food stamps or the use of a senior bus pass can make social ties easier to maintain. Small health aids such as hearing aids, glasses, or wheelchairs can often turn increasingly withdrawn, depressed elderly people into much more vibrant and concerned individuals. Assumptions that used to be made about the near inevitability of "senility" are inaccurate. "Senility" is essentially a general, imprecise term used to describe the effects of myriad physical, economic, and social disabilities. By treating the specific disability, the resultant "senility" can be averted.

Mary, Mother without a Role

Mary was a 70-year-old woman whose husband of 45 years had recently died. She had taken great pride in raising her three children and taking care of her home and family as a traditional housewife. However, her long history of alcohol abuse became even more evident after her husband's death, and she was unclear about her plans for the future.

"I don't want to live anymore," she explained to the social worker whom her physician had insisted that she see after a visit to the doctor. "My husband is dead. My kids are raised. I can't walk or see or hear well, and everybody keeps calling me an alcoholic. So what's there to live for?"

Only one of Mary's three children lived in the same city with her, and he had four young children of his own. Mary also had two brothers and two sisters who spoke with her regularly but were advanced in age themselves and indicated that Mary had become increasingly bitter and rarely answered her phone. Her son agreed to bring her in to see the social worker on a weekly basis in the evening. The first few sessions were used to let Mary ventilate her anger and hurt.

"You know, my husband really drank himself to death," she cried. "He just couldn't quit, and frankly I don't see any reason why I shouldn't do the same." Mary was depressed, discouraged, and had already chosen alcoholic consumption as her means of suicide. She had a severe case of osteoporosis, and she admitted to the social worker that she did not answer the phone because she could not hear it ring or could not find it or reach it in time if she did hear it because of her drinking and consequent immobility.

The social worker encouraged Mary to talk about her family. Her three children were fairly successful professional people who had compensated for their parents' alcoholism by striving for perfection and denying significant problems of their own. The older son was an alcoholic, but he nevertheless managed a successful law practice; the daughter was a social worker married to a psychiatrist; and the younger son had a doctorate in chemistry and directed research for a large corporation.

In assessing her social network, Mary perceptively stated that her children would really not be that much help. Two of them lived far away, and although she did not say so explicitly, it was apparent to her and the social worker that all three used a great deal of denial and that they also had some repressed anger toward their mother, which came out only indirectly in passive aggressive ways, such as not calling when they had promised or in sending gifts late on holidays.

Mary clarified her network and subsequent social support system to the social worker by describing her brothers and sisters. In spite of advancing age (Mary was the youngest of five, the other four ranging in age from 73 to 83), her siblings were very protective of Mary. Although the eldest sister disapproved of Mary's alcoholism to the extent that she would rarely speak with her, the others visited weekly and called daily. This process, which had begun after the death of Mary's husband, was encouraged strongly by the social worker. In fact, Mary's siblings began to come with Mary to several sessions.

The developing plan was to maintain and increase the visits by her three siblings, who also helped her with many routine chores around her apartment. The siblings also reinforced the social worker's suggestion that Mary's eyesight and hearing be retested and that she be seen again at a clinic that dealt with osteoporosis. She subsequently was given new eyeglasses, a hearing aid, and a walker. Because her siblings all used such devices themselves, they were able to help Mary accept and use them correctly.

Restructuring Mary's social support system involved going beyond the active support of her siblings and the addition of the needed physical aids. She needed to begin to go to Alcoholics Anonymous. She also needed to eat regularly and to become involved with activities outside her apartment. Mary admitted some concern about her lack of church attendance. She had been raised a Catholic and had been active in the church for many years but had not attended in three years. Mary confided to the social worker that she feared she would die without going to confession. After several discussions, a cousin of Mary who was a nun came for a visit, and together they called a local parish priest who agreed to visit Mary, hear her confession, and arrange for her to receive communion on a regular basis.

Finally, the social worker arranged for a woman from "Meals-on-Wheels" to bring in one well-balanced hot meal a day for her. This woman, who was an outgoing, jovial volunteer, responded to Mary's initial depressed cynicism with a very caring and supportive but clear message that Mary needed to do more for herself. This support plus the regular counseling from the social worker, who helped to develop and maintain the social support system, eventually served to significantly diminish the depression and suicidal tendencies. The alcoholism also significantly diminished but was not under control when the case was closed.

In working with Mary, the social worker had a very demanding case. This woman had lost her husband the previous year, and her three children had gradually grown away from her. She was fortunate to have a close-knit family of siblings who cared for her in spite of her frequent depression and hostility toward them. Her many health problems had been exacerbated by alcoholism, which also led to decreased mobility and thus lessened her capacity to maintain a social support system.

In spite of all of this, the social worker successfully broke the many problems into clear, discrete, manageable tasks. Mary was helped to get a walker, a hearing aid, and new glasses. She was further helped by going into a physical rehabilitation program to help with several broken bones related to osteoporosis. Perhaps most importantly, her brothers and sisters were encouraged to provide the needed social support to get her past her feelings of loss of her roles as traditional wife and mother. Efforts at getting her into treatment for alcoholism and to join Alcoholics Anonymous were less successful, so the prognosis was guarded.

Each life-stage provides new challenges. Social workers need to be knowledgeable of life-stage crises and developmental concerns. These issues make a significant difference in terms of the formation of social support systems. Clients in each stage of life need such systems, but relate to them differently because of their varying social needs and responsibilities. It is not enough to simply get people together. The social worker needs to know how and why some individuals should be included in a client's system, and some of this knowledge requires a background in the hopes, aspirations, demands, and problems of each of the stages of life.

Personal Retrospective of Life Crises Exercise

Instead of answering questions related to this chapter, do the following exercise on a sheet of paper with the five headings shown in the example. For those in their early 20s, a retrospective of the last 10 years or so is sufficient; for 30-year-olds, the last 15 years; for 40-year-olds, the last 20 or more; and for those in each additional decade, five more years should be added to the retrospective years.

1. Begin by picking any major life crisis, which we define as a significant task or event (for example, death, birth, major health problem for self or loved one).
2. Indicate the date (that is, the year or years) when the crisis or event occurred.
3. Give your age at the time of the crisis.
4. Briefly describe your attitudes and/or feelings related to the crisis or event.
5. Briefly describe your social support system and its responses.

Example

Task/Event	Year	Age	Attitudes/Feelings	Social Support System and Responses
Death of father	1983	16	Despair, loss, rejection, embarrassment, fear	Girlfriends, friends, or basketball team and church group. Women next door who spent hours listening, talking, holding.
College	1985–89	18–21	Socially: Fun, lots of new friends, regained confidence. First "serious" relationship. Lasted two years, mutual breakup.	Dormitory and, later, apartment roommates. Closer to mother, who became depressed, needy. New level of intimacy and honesty with boyfriend/girlfriend. Lots of group activities.

This exercise can be used in groups. After each individual (student or client) has completed it, the group can discuss the results while examining how and why, on the basis of age, race, sex, and socioeconomic status, the lists of critical events made up by the various group members differ.

References

Atchley, R. C. (1988). *Social forces and aging: An introduction to social gerontology* (5th ed.). Belmont, CA: Wadsworth.

Auslander, G., & Litwin, H. (1988). Social networks and the poor: Toward effective policy and practice. *Social Work, 3* (May/June), 234–238.

Fisher, B. (1981). *Rebuilding: When your relationship ends.* San Luis Obispo, CA: Impact.

Holahan, C. K. (1984). Marital attitudes over 40 years: A longitudinal and cohort analysis. *Journal of Gerontology, 39,* 49–57.

Kitson, G. C., & Raschke, H. J. (1981). Divorce research: What we know, what we need to know. *Journal of Divorce, 3,* 1–38.

Kreppner, K., & Lerner, R. M. (Eds.). (1989). *Family systems and life span development.* Hillsdale, NJ: Lawrence Erlbaum.

Lerner, J. V., & Lerner, R. M. (Eds.). (1986). *Temperament and social interaction in infants and children.* San Francisco: Jossey-Bass.

Lerner, R.M. (1984). *Experiencing adolescence: A sourcebook.* New York: Garland.

Lerner, R. M, & Galambos, N.L. (1984). *Experiencing adolescence: A sourcebook for parents, teachers, and teens.* New York: Garland.

Levinson, D. (1978). *Seasons of man's life.* New York: Knopf.

National Commission on Working Women. (1988). *No way out: Workers, poor women in the United States.* Washington, DC: U.S. Government Printing Office.

Shanas, E. (1979). The family as a social support system in old age. *The Gerontologist, 19,* 169–174.

Sheehy, G. (1976). *Passages: Preventable crises of adult life.* New York: Bantam.

Specht, R., & Craig, G. J. (1987). *Human development: A social work perspective* (2nd ed.). Englewood Cliffs, NJ: Prentice-Hall.

Sprenkle, D. H. (1985). *Divorce therapy.* New York: Haworth.

Sprenkle, D. H. (1988). *Treating issues related to divorce and separation.* Newbury Park, CA: Sage.

U.S. Bureau of the Census. (1983). *America in transition: An aging society—Current population reports* (Series P-23, No. 128). Washington, DC: U.S. Government Printing Office.

U.S. Senate Special Committee on Aging. (1986). *Developments in aging: 1985.* (Vol. 3). Washington, DC: U.S. Government Printing Office.

Weiss, R. (1975). *Marital separation.* New York: Basic Books.

Yamatani, H., Maguire, L., Rogers, R., & O'Kennedy, M. L. (in press). Battered families. In J. Cunningham & P. Martz (Eds.), *Family matters.* Pittsburgh: University of Pittsburgh Press.

Chapter 7

Applications of Social Support Systems: Past, Present, and Future

Past and Present Applications

This chapter begins by looking at the history of various past and present applications of social support systems and then examines three growing areas of concern that will affect social work practice in the future even more than they do now. Those areas are long-term mental illness, poverty and its effects, and AIDS (acquired immune deficiency syndrome).

The applied use of social support systems embodies and epitomizes social work practice. It is the essential component of what social workers do. The very name "social work" connotes a profession that works with and uses the social forces of individuals, families, and communities. This profession includes and uses knowledge related to changing social systems in its everyday work with clients.

The current and growing interest in using social support in practice is being generated by professionals who are not social workers, such as counselors and counselor educators (Pearson, 1990), as well as by psychologists, nurses, and social workers (Gottlieb, 1988), but this general social systems intervention approach is very much a social work model. It is a natural development of the work of Hollis (1981) and Perlman (1957), with later additions by Reid and Epstein (1972). It also grew from the ecological perspective of Germain and Gitterman (1980), who, along with Hartman and Laird (1983) in their family-oriented work, looked systematically at stress and social systems as they affect behavior and as forces in treatment.

The "best" of what social work has to offer avoids the extremes of rather intellectualized theoretical approaches to treatment, as occasionally practiced by psychoanalysts or Jungians. Social work also has fewer proponents of the purely behavioral scientific approach, which can lose the deeply significant subtleties of meaningful human existence for purposes of highly controlled quantification of only clearly observable behaviors. This is not to disparage either of these approaches. In fact, the social work profession not only borrows heavily from both but has also gained significantly from the theoretical paradigms and the methodological work developed in large part by other professions. Social work students, faculty, and practitioners can point with pride to a long history of mainstream social work approaches that borrow the best from others and at the same time maintain realistic, systems-oriented approaches to helping clients.

Recent social support system development follows in the practical tradition of the problem-solving approach of Perlman, the task-centered approach of Reid and Epstein, and the ecological approach of Germain and Gitterman. These approaches say that people have problems in their everyday interactions with the system. The system is composed of a social sphere that includes family, friends, work associates, neighbors, and organizations. This system in turn is affected by people's personal histories, personalities, cultures, societies, and learned patterns of behavior. As social workers, we must be consciously aware of changes in the system. Our treatment goals must involve modifying various aspects of whatever the individual brings into treatment as well as modifying that larger social support system, which affects him or her. The individual's personal worth and sense of self-esteem, mastery, and accomplishments are fortified through successful interactions with the system, and these successes can not only be maintained but generalized to include other, similar situations.

Social support systems in practice rely on the many practical applied social work approaches developed earlier, which begin with the personal verbal expression of the client's perceived views and concerns. The social worker then helps the client look at those issues in the context of what he or she brings to the process and in light of available resources (personal, financial, and so forth), as well as obstacles to improvement or change. Social support system development is similar to life itself: it is inherently complex, fascinating, and sometimes very difficult, yet manageable and highly rewarding when examined, clarified, and empathetically explored in its many, varied components.

It was my good fortune to have had Helen Harris Perlman for casework when I attended the University of Chicago. Professor Perlman was a warm, caring person whose style did not seem to fit her impressive intellect and depth and breadth of knowledge. Her students were mostly young and fresh out of college, and many of us expected a more arrogant, self-impressed, or somehow more intimidating figure than this diminutive, gentle but dynamic woman. As the year progressed, most learned from her that there is no great mystery to helping people solve problems—just a mixture of concern, good common sense, and knowledge of human behavior, in roughly that order.

I later sat in with and observed Laura Epstein working with the task-centered approach. Professor Epstein was seemingly more assertive, at least in behalf of her clients' needs, and took a very practical, down-to-earth approach with them. She was not overly interested in their past, just in what their two or three major present problems were and in what could be clearly and efficiently done for each one. She could be empathic while still keeping the clients to the clearly and narrowly defined task of alleviating their stated problems.

Years later, when I served as a consultant for the Council on Social Work Eduction, I had the pleasure of working with Carel Germain, who had collaborated very successfully with Alex Gitterman to develop the ecological approach. Once again I was struck by the fact that these individuals, who had given so much to the field of social work, were all practical, caring, "down-to-earth" people who seemed quite unimpressed with themselves or their accomplishments in spite of their output.

My own academic background has been in psychology as well as social work, but I have observed time and again that our colleagues in psychology and psychiatry, particularly the academicians, tend to be more comfortable with either the more purely theoretical or the purely "scientific" than are those of us in social work. Sociologists at times can be even more abstract, esoteric, and distant from practical human concerns than these other practitioners. Oddly enough, it is precisely this practical, realistic approach that in some circles has made social work less prestigious as a profession than the other areas. The fact that social work requires a master's degree rather than a doctorate as a standard terminal degree is another significant factor in such "ranking." But this "middle-of-the-road" approach to solving problems in the practical, realistic, day-to-day context of human interaction is the hallmark of social work practice and social support system development. Neither the highly intellectualized theoretical approaches nor the cold quantitative scientific interventions have gained the stronghold within social work that they occasionally have in other helping professions.

Perlman (1986) described her break with the traditional psychoanalytic approach, which dominated social work in the early days: "There was an all-but unquestioning acceptance of the iron determinism of the person's past and very little recognition of the moving forces in his current life experiences. Our interviewing focused upon the client's recounting of his problems, his history, along with the ventilation of the emotional freightage that accompanied them; our responses were compassionate and supportive, which often served some healing purposes, to be sure, but scarcely prepared the client for grappling with his present-day difficulties" (p. 248).

Perlman's departure from the psychoanalytic perspective also came at a time when social work was developing a "functionalist" approach (sometimes called Rankian), which espoused many of the practical ideas later adopted by Perlman and others. Among these developing ideas were the following:

- A focus on the here and now, which formed the later basis for both crisis intervention and the Rogerian approach

- The impact of the agency itself, or the setting and how it affects clients

- The importance of the relationship and its use in practice, and related qualities such as trust, responsiveness, and warmth

- The notion that timing of treatment is essential, and that interventions must have a beginning, a middle, and an end— a concept that departed from the traditional, long-term, insight-oriented therapies and set the stage for short-term, planned treatment

- Partialization (that is, the need to break down vague or complex ideas into clear, discrete, manageable problems), which has subsequently been supported in social psychological research and training research as an important component of effective and efficient changes (Perlman, 1986).

The *psychosocial approach* to social work practice merits special attention, because it is often considered the general dominant theory for social workers as well as being an approach that is unique to our profession. In general, the term applies to any approach that recognizes the balance of psychological and social-environmental factors relevant to thoughts and behavior. More specifically, it refers to an approach in social work that was progressively developed by people such as Mary Richmond, Gordon Hamilton, Betsy Libby, Bertha Reynolds, Annette Garrett, and particularly Florence Hollis.

Psychosocial theory refers to the perspective that stresses an integrated focus—not only on intrapsychic phenomena and past developmental issues but also on current issues and stresses such as economic or peer pressure or family dynamics. It incorporates many of the concepts relevant to crisis theory, family theory, learning theory, and systems theory. It also stresses the need for social workers to recognize interpersonal, intrapersonal, and intersystemic factors. Furthermore, it requires that the client look both outward and inward and reflect on the interconnectedness of the two (Turner, 1986).

The psychosocial approach is extremely broad. Some may have considered it so expansive as to be too vague or nebulous as a foundation for practice. They may feel that by trying to cover and consider so much, it loses specificity of focus itself. However, the psychosocial approach has probably received even more validation in recent years *because* of its comprehensiveness.

Psychiatry, clinical psychology, nursing, and various rehabilitation and counseling approaches have begun to take up this traditional social work focus on social and environmental factors as the identified causes of and treatments for select problems. In fact, few mental health practitioners of any profession could defend their practices today without a clear acceptance of the general principles of the social systems or at least the psychosocial approach. Since at least the 1950s, the field of social work has had as its anchor this psychosocial orientation, at the same time maintaining a firm foundation in the practical understanding of environmental impacts on thoughts, feelings, and behavior. The future will probably lie in learning how to use these social-environmental forces better in treating people or otherwise helping them solve their own problems.

Future Applications

Long-Term Mental Illness

The care of chronically mentally ill people has been central to social work and particularly the community mental health field for many years. The major theme of public mental health policy has been deinstitutionalization, and it has increasingly generated a substantial literature as well as a great deal of public attention throughout society.

The problems that demand the attention of social workers who care for chronically mentally ill people in the future are many. First, individuals suffering from severe mental disabilities are characterized by a wide range of disabilities and service needs that are often lifelong conditions. In sharp contrast to the breadth and variety of these needs, service delivery tends too often to be brief and noncontinuous, with a view toward quick change. With respect to chronically mentally ill people, many community-based programs place unwarranted emphasis on the brief and episodic user of services, and this tends to underservice people with lifelong disorders.

A second problem for social workers will be that many programs ostensibly designed as deinstitutionalization programs resist treating those individuals who are most severely impaired and thus are not realistically directed toward the needs of these people (Link & Milcarek, 1980). Often the chronic patient cannot use the current mental health system because it was developed for people who have the motivation, or at least the capacity, to develop insights and change behaviors. These characteristics are not generally, or at least not universally, descriptive of the long-term mentally ill. Furthermore, in most instances there is a reversed system of care in which the most trained and skilled clinicians deal with the most articulate, interesting, and likely-to-succeed clientele, whereas the problems of those most in need are left largely to students in training or to the less-trained staff.

A third problem is that the delivery of community-based services to the long-term mentally impaired takes place against a backdrop of stigma exceedingly difficult to overcome. People often fear and avoid the long-term mentally ill. Deinstitutionalization has only served in larger cities to antagonize many people, who look upon the homeless mentally ill wandering the streets as frightening and potentially dangerous eyesores.

Fourth, the fragmentation of services and authority in addressing the needs of long-term mentally disabled people is a serious and difficult problem that has the effect of reducing the quality of care. In past years most persons with chronic mental disabilities were admitted to large institutions where most remained, often for the rest of their lives. They represented an essentially static population pool that changed primarily as a result of new admissions and deaths. Providing care was relatively simple: Virtually all services could be delivered within a single physical setting. Today, by contrast, authority for providing for the needs of disabled persons is divided among numerous health, educational, and human services agencies in the public and private sectors. Successful deinstitutionalization programs require the fine-tuning of initiatives that originate with separate, sometimes competing, authorities—a process far more complicated than was suggested in President John F. Kennedy's "bold new approach" to service provision back in 1963. Improved coordination of services and case management techniques are obvious answers to this problem, but until such skills become a central part of the education of all social workers, many long-term mentally disabled people will continue suffering.

The fifth problem that will affect social workers working with the long-term mentally ill in the future is that deinstitutionalization programs are designed and implemented within a context of semantic confusion that both reflects and sustains service delivery problems. This conceptual vagueness is a potent barrier to effective care, and it underscores a general failure to assess adequately the many issues related to deinstitutionalization. Deinstitutionalization has resulted in myriad political, psychological, social, and economic problems, which subsequently translates into approaches to the problem that reflect each of these specialties. Social work as a profession is relatively well suited to dealing with such broad-based problems, given its historical base in each of these areas. Yet even social workers are often unclear as to whether this problem should be defined and managed from a political, economic, psychological, or sociological approach.

The needs of chronically mentally ill people highlight the need for a strong cadre of mental health professionals with clinical skills sensitive to both the individual problems and the strengths of the social network of their long-term mentally ill patients. Yet their skills must go beyond that. A clear understanding of the community networks and support systems must also be a significant part of the interventive repertoire of clinical social workers.

One of the key issues in this area that must be given the most thoughtful attention is the necessity of a continuum of services— including careful preparation of institutionalized patients for entry into the community and the availability of sources of support, both informal and formal, if the long-term mentally ill are to be helped to maintain their social functioning within the community. Because the demands on the service dollar and resources have continued to increase but available resources have not, it becomes even clearer that the approach of choice must include central emphasis on the use of informal social support systems and networks.

Social workers are among the leading figures in the planning and provision of the types of services that enhance social functioning, so it is vital that social work practitioners be educated to work with this focus. They must be taught to bring new and old skills and knowledge into the planning and program development as well as into the service delivery systems that are serving chronically mentally ill people. The importance of the planned use of supportive networks cannot be emphasized enough: it is very clear that deinstitutionalization cannot work properly if these systems are not included.

Furthermore, without considerable use of networks and natural support systems, the mental health service delivery system cannot cope with the tremendous number of chronically mentally ill patients. Their numbers in this country are overwhelming. Based on the report of the President's Commission on Mental Health (1978), there are approximately 2 million people in the United States who could be diagnosed as schizophrenic. Approximately 600,000 of them are in active treatment during a given year, accounting for more than 500,000 admissions in the specialty mental health sector. Any individual given a diagnosis of schizophrenia is at risk of becoming a long-term mentally ill patient. However, because other acute syndromes mimic the overt symptoms of schizophrenia but do not invariably become progressive or chronic (for example, schizophreniform psychosis, acute psychotic episode), not all of the 2 million individuals are to be counted among the chronically mentally ill population. Estimates of the number of chronically mentally ill individuals with a diagnosis of schizophrenia would range from 500,000 to 900,000.

Also according to the report of the President's Commission, serious depression has a prevalence rate ranging from 0.3 percent to 1.2 percent. Assuming that the lower end of the range represents the population at highest risk of chronicity, there are perhaps 600,000 to 800,000 chronically and severely depressed individuals in the United States. Furthermore, psychosis in the elderly (primarily organic brain syndrome, predominantly chronic) is estimated to account for between 600,000 and 1,250,000 individuals.

Other more prevalent disorders, such as personality disorders (7.0 percent prevalence), alcoholism and alcohol abuse (5 to 10 percent), and drug abuse and misuse (1 to 10 percent, depending on the type of drug) may become chronic or may be complicated by chronic mental disorder. However, only a small minority of these individuals is being adequately served (American Psychiatric Association, 1987; Main, 1983; President's Commission on Mental Health, 1978).

Community mental health centers and the community mental health movement were taking a large share of the blame for unresponsiveness to a problem they did not create. Like the asylum and psychopathic hospitals before them, the centers did fail to meet the idealized expectations of the reformers who introduced them. In each case it was the difficulty of curing the long-term patient that led to disillusionment.

This disillusionment with services provided to the long-term mentally ill has occurred on numerous occasions in the past. In the United States, there have been at least three major reform movements and reform institutions. The first cycle of reform introduced moral treatment and the asylum, the second generated the mental hygiene movement and the psychopathic hospital, and the third created the community mental health movement and the community mental health center. A fourth reform, associated with networks and community support systems, has more recently developed within the mental health professions, and social support systems are central elements in this hope for the future (President's Commission on Mental Health, 1978; Turner & Ten Hoor, 1978).

There appears to be a consensus among social workers and other mental health professionals that supportive care in the least restrictive environment is of most benefit to the long-term mentally ill, as well as to their families and society in general. Furthermore, there is a developing consensus that the use of natural helping networks and the social support provided by kith and kin must be better understood in order to make treatment, prevention, and rehabilitation both more effective and more humane.

Schizophrenics and Social Support

Patricia was a 38-year-old married woman with two children. She had been diagnosed as schizophrenic at age 18 and had been hospitalized on four occasions since that time, with stays in the hospital that averaged two months.

James, her husband of 15 years, was a recovering alcoholic who was a leader of the local Alcoholics Anonymous (AA) group. He had initially gone to the community mental health center (CMHC) to discuss a possible arrangement with the social worker about helping him develop AA groups in this small town, but his own personal agenda was his wife. He distrusted social workers and personally felt that, although they were more understanding than psychiatrists or psychologists, they were still ill-informed.

Finding that the social worker was extremely helpful and supportive and had many good ideas as well as potential referrals for

*him for AA, James reluctantly began to speak of his wife and his real
reason for coming to the CMHC.*

*"My wife Pat is a wonderful, beautiful person. She took care of
me when I was a useless drunk, but sometimes she's absolutely crazy.
She's on some sort of medication that helps a lot. She got it about two
years ago when she left the state hospital. The doc there sees her
every four months when he renews her prescription."*

*The social worker was surprised not to know of this woman in a
town of only 6,000 people, but she soon learned that Pat and her
husband were basically treating the schizophrenia through a 12-step
self-help concept similar to AA's. Although this can be very supportive
in a group setting and in conjunction with a self-help organization
such as Recovery, Incorporated, its merits are questionable in
isolation.*

*Once convinced that the social worker was acceptable, James
brought Pat in to see her. Pat's condition was deteriorating; she was
noticeably paranoid, agitated, depressed, and disoriented. She had
been taking the antipsychotic medication sporadically, but it was
insufficient to stop her condition from deteriorating further. After two
more sessions within 48 hours, it was apparent that she needed to
return to the hospital to improve and stabilize her condition.*

*The social worker at the CMHC made the arrangements for Pat
to be admitted to a good local hospital that had a small psychiatric
ward. The state hospital, which was 200 miles away, was
overcrowded, understaffed, and generally antagonistic to the CMHC.
The level of communication between the two facilities had been poor
for many years. The new local hospital's psychiatric ward was
innovative, committed to working with social workers and community
groups, and was known for excellent follow-up and joint efforts. The
social worker went with Pat and her husband to arrange the
hospitalization and introduced them both to several members of the
hospital staff.*

*Pat was honestly reassured that she would be able to continue
seeing the CMHC social worker after she left the hospital and even
while she was a patient. Furthermore, the center social worker called
the medical assistance case worker to manage payment for
hospitalization and referred Pat and her family to a visiting nurse.
The visiting nurse was a public-health-trained registered nurse whose
background was in psychiatry. She later visited the home on a weekly
basis for a medication check and to help Pat with her children.*

*While Pat was still in the hospital, her husband and the CMHC
social worker worked with her to develop a self-help group in the*

community that worked along the lines of the 12-step framework. This altruistic, outwardly-oriented activity served to focus Pat's energy on a positive goal that could also potentially serve as a major source of social support.

The social support approach exemplified in the preceding case was rather typical of case management in that it was managed by a social worker at a CMHC with good community contacts and a strong belief in informal as well as formal social supports. The visiting public health nurse, the hospital's psychiatrist, and the hospital social worker were all kept informed about and involved with Pat's progress and stability through the CMHC social worker even after Pat had left the hospital following her short, 30-day hospitalization. Pat developed a Recovery, Incorporated, chapter locally with the support of each of the professionals and with the benefit of her husband's experience from AA. The ties with the geographically distant rural state psychiatric hospital were severed, although that institution supplied an excellent and detailed history of Pat's hospitalization, medication, and tests. They welcomed the opportunity to refer their patient to a local hospital that could keep Pat close to her family, friends, and multiple supportive helping professionals.

Poverty and Its Effects

A primary focus of the social work profession has been poverty and its effects, such as homelessness and lack of opportunities for individuals, families, and communities. Without adequate financial resources, people cannot provide for themselves the fundamental needs of life such as food and shelter. In the United States, the wealthiest nation in the world, millions of people—many of whom are children—are poor and homeless. Of the 35 million poor in the United States, 13 million are children, and 500,000 of these children are homeless (Kozol, 1990). Homelessness itself has been found to have profound psychological effects on children. The tragedy is compounded by the fact that many of them will grow up in neighborhoods or rural areas where they learn to accept and live with the effects of poverty— malnutrition, sickness, disease, homelessness, and the even greater tragedies of despair and loss of hope for the future.

Macro Orientation to Addressing the Problem. This tragedy of poverty and its effects in the United States originates as a macro socioeconomic phenomenon. Our culture has accepted a rather

Darwinian approach toward individuals economically in that the socially, educationally, and financially "strong" survive and prosper while the "weak" become weaker or even more poverty-stricken. The disparity between the rich and poor in this country has grown alarmingly large, and the resources available to help the poor are equally alarming in their scarcity.

Within this broad and diverse field known as the social work profession, two general camps have evolved over the years: the micro practitioners and the macro practitioners—those who deal with the effects of poverty and those who deal with the causes of poverty. Although both groups recognize the need for the eradication of poverty, both also recognize that it has been with us in this and basically all other cultures throughout the ages. This may not change and in fact has been even worse in some "civilized" eras in the past, for example, in Great Britain's early industrial period, described so eloquently by Charles Dickens. Poverty and its effects also exist today in many Third World countries whose vast majority live in abject poverty while an extremely small number of elite families control most of their country's wealth.

Social support systems are relevant to the macro orientation toward poverty because they can apply to us as professionals, individuals, and social workers. That is, social workers need to provide support to *each other* to develop systems of organized practitioners who attack the problem of poverty from a political and policy-oriented perspective. As individuals they can do relatively little to affect political policy. As organized professionals who talk with each other and who share opinions, facts, and strategies for changing policies relevant to poverty, social workers can and must become political forces that provide social support systems to each other.

At this point the macro orientation of social work practice to social support systems development involves the use of four general approaches, each of which focuses on the causes of poverty: political action and lobbying, coalition development, local education and consultation, and grassroots organization.

Politicians respond to organized efforts of large groups of constituents. If they are made aware of the fact that a significant number of politically active voters and organizers favors or is against poverty-related legislation, they respond. Through political action and lobbying, social workers must get to know and work with local, state, and national elected officials and their staffs. From a macro perspective, social support system intervention involves their working within the political system and lobbying. It requires that social workers become involved with the politicians and policy planners of their localities, regions, and states and with national organizations. NASW has taken an active leadership role in this movement through PACE (Political Action for Candidate Election) and through the National Center for Social Policy and Practice, both of which are sustained through support from practitioners.

When organized groups of professionals further augment their resources by combining their abilities and memberships with each other, they can develop new, innovative, and powerful ways of attacking the causes of economic disadvantages. *Coalition development* from the social support system perspective involves meeting with other social workers and with a variety of other groups, such as poverty-oriented organizations, other professional organizations, and other groups that are involved with or affected by poverty. Social support systems by their nature imply active combinations and linkages of people. In this instance, smaller groups join forces to move powerful systems that support each other in pursuit of a larger cause—the eradication of policies and political actions that negatively affect the economically disadvantaged.

Local education and consultation involve educating communities, organizations, families, and individuals about the causes and effects of poverty. Studies have found that some populations, such as single women and minorities, do indeed suffer disproportionately from economic disadvantage—for example, from unemployment— and subsequently suffer greater emotional harm, particularly depression (Yamatani, Maguire, Rogers, & Martz, in press). When people are better informed about how and why poverty affects them directly, they are more motivated to become actively involved in changing policy—or politicians—who are not supportive of them.

Social workers need to provide expert consultation to neighborhood groups, local PTAs, block-watch programs against crime, civil rights organizations, and other organized systems to provide the facts and substantiate the needs for change, because social systems are more supportive when they have facts available. When organized groups attack the causes of poverty and homelessness such as racism, hunger, bias, poor school systems, and lack of employment opportunities or even training, they must do so in a planned fashion. Facts and figures are useful weapons in confronting politicians and policymakers. Firmly confronting local politicians and directors of agencies also adds considerable credibility to these coalitions.

Grassroots organizations include some of the informal local organizations mentioned above, as well as organized groups of concerned local individuals. A macro orientation to social systems development in this arena requires community organization skills, such as knowing the local problems and the local leadership well. It requires social workers to listen and learn from these groups and then to help them use their strongest assets and resources to overcome the problem being addressed. In short, it is the same process used frequently with individuals in counseling, the difference being that in this type of situation the social worker goes after the causes of the problem on a larger social scale rather than dealing with its effects on an individual or familial scale.

If the crime rate is escalating in a block or section of a neighborhood, for instance, social workers need to canvas residents, establish the perceived cause of the problem, and mobilize untapped resources to deal with those causes. Many local problems can be best addressed by local residents. There are many examples of local-area residents who have appealed unsuccessfully to police or formal agencies to tear down abandoned, rat-infested buildings or to investigate houses where drugs were sold or prostitution flourishes. After a critical mass of local people developed or when they found a leader, these same residents have occasionally found it more expedient (although potentially more dangerous) to confront the problem themselves at the grassroots level. Inattentive politicians and drug dealers have few viable responses to large groups of local people who picket or block doorways of such illegal operations.

Such grassroots displays can also be used to gain media attention to the lack of housing and the need for rehabilitation of older housing in deteriorating communities. Finding the answers to homelessness, poverty, poor schools, crimes, and other large-scale societal problems can be accomplished by using the same five basic stages described in chapter 2 for social support system interventions. First, the worker gets community residents and concerned citizens to ventilate and discuss their problems in open public meetings. Next, a developing committee assesses the extent of the problem in the community. Further clarification of the problem and the scope should ensue, leading to the planning stage. After carefully planning what needs to be done and how to do it, the committee proceeds to act by restructuring the system. That is, it takes action by confronting or demanding change from politicians, school officials, police, or housing planners in the community.

Micro Orientation to Problems of Poverty. Micro orientation to
poverty involves working with individuals and families to deal with its
psychological effects—including homelessness, unemployment, poor
health care, inadequate schools, disrupted families, crime, and a
myriad of other social problems.

The role of deficient economic resources in the psychological
equation is not that of a pure, simple, causal variable. In other words,
being poor does not cause despair or depression, nor does it "force"
anyone—or one's children or spouse—to commit crimes or abuse
drugs or alcohol. The profession of social work has gone beyond the
naiveté of earlier decades to recognize that social support systems and
planning, not just more money, can dramatically mitigate the possible
effects of economic disadvantage. There are too many examples of
poor but well-adjusted, highly functioning black families in the rural
South or urban North to hypothesize a causal relationship between
poverty and major psychosocial maladjustment. Immigrant Asian
groups with almost no money have shown in recent generations that
the close bonds of caring, motivated families can lead to well-adjusted
children who become highly successful by virtually any standard. Still
other examples exist on today's Indian reservations, where there may
be insufficient food and perhaps shelter with only a dirt floor, but
where families care for and nourish each other and provide support for
one another that leads to quiet dignity, self-assurance, and a caring
nature that cannot be bought with any amount of money.

But whatever the examples that can be given in this never-ending
debate, the fact is that crime rates are higher, health statistics are
lower, and insufficient housing is endemic in poor areas. Furthermore,
the social forces correlated with poverty cannot help having a negative
effect on most families. For instance, the youngster who is the product
of a rough, dangerous, drug-infested inner-city school may indeed find
himself or herself unprepared, even after high school, to achieve the
training or education needed to break out of poverty. It is this loss of
human resources—where social support systems are overwhelmed or
incapable of counteracting the many effects of poverty—that is tragic.

The micro orientation to poverty focuses on its effects. Although
there is no clear causal relationship between poverty and adverse
psychological or even behavioral responses, poverty never exists in
isolation. It affects individuals and families by undermining self-
esteem and confidence, which are partially based on the ability to
adequately protect, defend, feed, shelter, and clothe oneself. Without
the real and perceived capacity to provide these basic necessities of
life, certain psychological responses generally ensue. For instance,

despair and lethargy, which are both major symptoms of depression, are likely reactions when one realistically assesses his or her future plans and finds them to be hopeless. The homeless, the illiterate, and the chronically ill who also lack sufficient social support systems have legitimate cause for such despair.

Social workers dealing with individuals and families mired in the effects of poverty cannot merely provide psychotherapy or counseling. That is clearly insufficient. Social support system intervention with the chronically poor, or what some call the underclass, necessitates taking action to deal with the poverty-related factors that cause the stress, depression, anger, or "deviant" behavior.

Often, a homeless, unemployed woman or man suffers additionally from emotional problems such as depression or, in many instances, long-term disorders such as alcoholism or schizophrenia. Whatever the psychological and/or addictive disorder may be, part of the response of the social worker will be the same: to provide a stable social support system.

The system for a poor client will involve getting housing and jobs, supporting, guiding, and occasionally directing him or her to sources of potential housing or employment as part of the healing process of treatment. As experienced social workers who have worked with the long-term poor know, the priority of services frequently becomes the provision of the most basic need. Fortunately, by actively engaging the client in pursuing new housing or job opportunities, the worker also works against the lethargy and despair that accompany long-term homelessness and unemployment. The mere fact of having the client suggest and pursue leads, with the worker's help, invariably keeps the client out of the circular loop of despair. Typically, this involves the loss of a job, which leads to a loss of housing, which leads to poor health, disorientation, and despair. By providing hope in the form of leads, followed by active referral and contacts, the loop of despair can gradually be broken and the road to economic as well as psychological well-being can be found.

Mildred: Homeless and Lost in the System

Mildred was a 56-year-old divorced woman who had been living in the streets and at short-term shelters for nearly two months. She was brought in to see the social worker by a policeman who had worked with the social worker at the downtown branch of Catholic

Social Services. The policeman explained that he had seen Mildred walking around the downtown area for several weeks and had twice stopped teenagers from harassing her. He observed that Mildred was apparently deteriorating mentally and physically, and he feared that she would be seriously hurt or die if she did not get some help. He was uncertain about whether the social worker could (or would) help, but he knew that jail was inappropriate and no hospital would take her.

Mildred apprehensively walked into the office clutching a large purse and holding a shopping bag. She wore several layers of clothing and had not washed or bathed for days. She relaxed slightly after the policeman left, but her fear of the social worker and the office was clear. The social worker tried to make Mildred feel at ease and explained that their agency was there to help anyone in need.

"I'm okay," was Mildred's only response, and that was said in a barely audible tone directed at the floor. The social worker pointed out that Mildred had a large bruise on her hand and asked if she had received any medical attention for it.

"No. They don't want me in there no more," she said, "I been to the hospital a couple times after some kids beat me up, and the hospital people told me to stay away—and to get a place to live."

"That sounds pretty rough. Where are you living now?" asked the social worker.

"Well, sometimes underneath the Ninth Street Bridge, but some bad kids hang around there now, so I stay away. I stop at the shelter most nights," Mildred explained.

The social worker began this session in a warm, nonthreatening, supportive but relatively concrete fashion. She felt that Mildred could relate more comfortably, at least initially, to general questions about housing, and later about food. Mildred was extremely guarded and looked ready to run from the office, so the worker slowly and gradually worked up to the other issues.

Mildred explained that she had been married for about 20 years and had two children, but she had no contact with them. They had been taken from her one of the times she was in the state hospital during a schizophrenic episode. She said that the pills she had received in the past at the CMHC made her dizzy, and she did not feel she needed them any longer.

The social worker called the therapist at the CMHC and explained that Mildred was with her and had been living mostly on the streets for two months. She had Mildred speak to her therapist on the phone. It became apparent to the social worker that the therapist she had just called was only marginally familiar with Mildred and viewed *her as a "chronic" with little hope for change. Their relationship had consisted of "med checks," at which they would have brief discussions, and then medications would be renewed or the dosage modified.*

The social worker then took the telephone from Mildred and told the CMHC therapist that Mildred was physically at risk and was in need of immediate shelter in a protected therapeutic environment. The therapist reluctantly agreed to see if one of their halfway houses or partial-care facilities would have an opening.

After hanging up, the social worker spoke with Mildred and found that, in spite of her slight disorientation and paranoia (which at least partially may have reflected reality), Mildred was otherwise lucid and even motivated by fear to get off the streets. Mildred was well aware of her diagnosis, and even described having "good months and bad months," acknowledging that the medication she received from the CMHC did help her in some ways. She agreed to take one of her pills, which she carried with her, in the social worker's office. As they waited for the return call, the social worker discussed the need for staying on the medication and spoke of the advantages of living in one of the facilities run by the CMHC.

The therapist called back, said that there was emergency space available for a few days at a halfway house, and that she would visit Mildred there that evening. There was no guarantee of housing after four or five days, but if Mildred agreed to get back on her medication and otherwise to abide by the restrictions of the halfway house, they might be able to find her permanent, or at least longer-term, housing at a house that also provided some therapeutic help.

The problem of homelessness will no doubt be with us for many years. The homeless are a population with few advocates and many needs. Among its members are alcoholics, schizophrenics, and a growing number of individuals who have been forced onto the streets because of economic and social forces beyond their control. This tragedy is particularly unfortunate in that a growing segment of this group consists of young adults and children whose hopes for the future and productivity for themselves and others grow weaker with each day they remain on the streets.

AIDS

AIDS has become the most tragic killer of modern times. Together with other conditions such as AIDS-related complex (ARC) associated with the human immunodeficiency virus (HIV), AIDS has become a disease of major proportions that affects precisely the populations that social work has professed to help—yet that help has been slow. AIDS has disproportionately affected minorities of color and sexual preference and the poor. Many argue that the poor, and particularly homosexuals and drug abusers, are being passively punished by a conservative and relatively hostile society by having care withheld from them. Benign neglect and passive indifference have marked much of the nation's attitude toward treatment and research.

Ryan (1991) has indicated that the profession of social work has been deficient in its response to the AIDS epidemic. She contends that the profession has not prepared enough social workers to deal with AIDS, and that even those who are trained are often not members of the affected minorities or cultures. There is not enough training on this subject in schools of social work, and many students and practitioners still admit to being very fearful and uncomfortable working with AIDS sufferers. Relatively few agencies have adapted to the high degree of stress and potential for burnout associated with working with this population. For instance, extremely high caseloads still exist where AIDS patients are treated no differently from anyone else. Support groups for staff members are few, so that social workers attempting to deal with AIDS end up feeling overwhelmed and hopeless. Social and familial problems further exacerbate the obvious health and psychological devastation experienced by AIDS sufferers. The children of AIDS victims also suffer, with more than 10,000 children in New York City alone having lost one or both parents to the disease. As a result of all this, many social workers have turned away from work with this population, which is perceived as dangerous, low in status, demanding, and personally and professionally overwhelming.

AIDS patients are also prone to depression because of the social stigma that many continue to attach to the disease. It is still considered to be the disease of homosexuals and drug users, two groups that have been shunned by many in the mainstream of society. Even the families of AIDS sufferers who are willing and able to continue to support and care for their loved ones are eventually unable to provide the specific knowledge and expertise needed to answer some questions, let alone deal with the fear of death that stalks all AIDS sufferers.

In assessing a family's willingness to care for a member with AIDS, three separate areas must be examined: emotional support, instrumental support, and physical support (McDonell, Abel, and

Miller, 1991). Emotionally, families are required to deal simultaneously with their own fear of loss and to help the sufferer deal with his or her fears and day-to-day problems. In terms of the instrumental support, the families need to be able to provide meals, transportation, and housecleaning, and to perform other tasks that may become impossible for their family members. Physically, families and family members need to be asked about their own capacity to bathe or change the sheets for their loved one or help him or her in and out of bed. Realistically, many families are incapable of providing all of these services even when the love and commitment are present. However, given the fact that nonfamily supports tend to decline and social networks become increasingly small, dense, and familial with a long-term degenerative illness such as AIDS (Wolcott, Namir, Fawzy, Gottlieb, & Mitsuyasu, 1986), it is essential that the family become involved, whenever possible, with ongoing care and support.

In summary, social support system intervention with AIDS patients is generally carried out through the family directly, through organized support groups, or through the formal system of medical and social services specifically designed to deal with AIDS and HIV.

The family is the first line of defense and also, as is the case with schizophrenics, the last to leave. However, also like schizophrenics, AIDS sufferers may have alienated their families in the past through behaviors of which the families disapproved, or they may simply have no close family ties. Where these ties do exist, the psychosocial assessment such as that developed by McDonell et al. (1991) is strongly recommended. As in other social support system interventions, such careful assessments of available resources, levels of willingness, and possible impediments to assistance all need to be addressed. The families themselves will undoubtedly need continued support from the social worker in the form of information about the disease and about its progress and symptoms, as well as other available social service, health, and psychiatric supports.

After families, support groups comprise the second major type of social support system resource available to AIDS sufferers. Such groups provide opportunities for catharsis and for open expression of fears and hopes, which are the first steps in assessing and understanding the depth of the problem. By meeting with others who share the problem, understand its results, and empathize with those having the same fears and concerns as their own, group members can look more realistically at AIDS. Too often, well-meaning family and friends try to minimize the problem to "protect" their relative or loved one.

Groups are less likely to do this, particularly when facilitated by an experienced social group worker who knows that the members need to open up, express their anger and fear, and hear from others who are similarly afflicted. Universality, which is a therapeutic factor found in such groups, allows members to realize that they are not alone but that they are part of a caring group that understands what they are suffering. This type of support, buttressed by the equally therapeutic factor of altruism, helps members realize they are still worthy of love and respect. The sharing of information about the disease and its progress, the socialization opportunities, and the chance to learn more about themselves through interpersonal interactions with peers are all important therapeutic factors in groups such as these (Yalom, 1985).

Approaches that deal specifically with the devastating loss of social support suffered by most AIDS victims need to be developed. As indicated above, one of the most efficient and effective ways of developing social support for AIDS is through support groups, which counteract the feeling of isolation, provide support and information, serve as an antidote to depression and hopelessness, and put some degree of control over decisions back into the hands of those affected. Support groups also help to provide socials outlets for men and women who may have been abandoned by their former social systems (Getzel, 1991).

As described by Getzel (1991), four specific types of solutions using group processes were identified among AIDS support groups:

1. The beneficient solution, which is characterized by members' performing loving and caring actions as a way of being remembered after death or as a way of undoing some personal flaw

2. The heroic solution, in which members see themselves as symbolic representatives of the contest with death, so they try to make their remaining lives rich in symbolic meaning, often through statements of belief

3. The artistic/spiritual solution, which involves members who view themselves as somehow "enduring beyond death through a leap of faith or an aesthetic depiction of immortality."

4. The rational instrument solution, which focuses on practical, day-to-day needs and on how to make decisions and choices through knowledge, precedent, convention, and the members' own expertise.

Others have researched the use of groups for AIDS sufferers (Child & Getzel, 1989; Gambe & Getzel, 1989) and found that small formal support groups are among the most therapeutic means available, particularly for their capacity to provide the needed social support of fellow sufferers. Such groups allow and encourage members to ventilate their understandable fears, which can become paralyzing and devastating when left unexpressed. The isolated AIDS patient is cut off from the hope gained through knowledge and any positive experiences of others. Realistic assessment of the problem and plans for the future are virtually impossible for the AIDS sufferer who is isolated and facing many profound losses (Mandel, 1986).

The last source of social support for AIDS sufferers involves the coordinated utilization of the formal system of doctors, nurses, social workers, and counselors in an efficient, positive unit. Social support system intervention in the form of coordinated case management is essential for these patients. Because the effects of AIDS are not only devastating but far-reaching in their health, mental health, social, economic, and even political consequences, capable management skills are needed. Also needed are knowledge of the types of service available from these many potential resources and further knowledge of the ability and willingness of those providing these resources to work with AIDS patients.

Many social workers working with the AIDS population have found that even fellow social workers in traditional agencies are sometimes reluctant to offer their services or to become too involved. This reluctance can be minimized only through education and the realization that AIDS patients need and deserve help and, with appropriate precautions, are no more of a risk to the clinician personally than are other clients with contagious diseases.

Questions

1. What other problems or populations exist that you see as needing social support system intervention? What specific and unique characteristics exist for this problem or population that will present special challenges to the social worker? Why? How will these challenges be overcome?

2. Poverty of some sort has existed in all modern industrial societies. How realistic are the approaches suggested to ameliorate poverty? If you feel they are inadequate or

unrealistic, how would you modify some of the suggested approaches? (*Note:* The option of giving up or saying it cannot be changed is not an accepted choice.)

3. Schizophrenics are sometimes described as being incapable of forming ongoing, intimate ties because of their faulty perceptions of reality and their erratic and unpredictable behavior. Compare social support system intervention to traditional individual or group therapy as a way to counteract these concerns. Which is best? Why?

4. What are the main problems you personally would have in using social support systems for AIDS sufferers? What are your own fears? What is the basis for that fear?

References

American Psychiatric Association. (1987). *Diagnostic and statistical manual of mental disorders* (3rd ed., rev.). Washington, DC: Author.

Child, R., & Getzel, G. S. (1989). Group work with inner city people with AIDS. *Social Work with Groups, 12,* 65–80.

Gambe, R., & Getzel, G. S. (1989). Group work with gay men with AIDS. *Social Casework, 70,* 172–179.

Germain, C. B., & Gitterman, A. (1980). *The life model of social work practice.* New York: Columbia University Press.

Getzel, G. S. (1991). Survival modes for people with AIDS in groups. *Social Work, 36* (1), 7–11.

Gottlieb, B. (Ed.). (1988). *Marshalling social support: Formats, processes and effects.* Newbury Park, CA: Sage.

Hartman, A., & Laird, J. (1983). *Family-centered social work practice.* New York: Free Press.

Hollis, F. (1981). *Casework: A psychosocial therapy* (3rd ed.). New York: Random House.

Kozol, J. (1990). The new untouchables. *Newsweek: Special edition.* Winter/Spring.

Link, B., & Milcarek, B. (1980). Selection factors in the dispensation of therapy: The Matthew effect in the allocation of mental health services. *Journal of Health and Social Behavior, 21,* 279–290.

Main, T. J. (1983). The homeless of New York City. *The Public Interest, 72* (Summer), 3–28.

Mandel, J. (1986). Psychosocial challenges of AIDS and ARC: Clinical and research observations. In L. McKusick (Ed.), *What to do about AIDS* (pp. 75–86). Berkeley, CA: University of California Press.

McDonell, J. R., Abel, N., & Miller, J. (1991). Family members' willingness to care for people with AIDS: A psychosocial assessment model. *Social Work, 36* (1), 43–53.

Pearson, R. E. (1990). *Counseling and social support: Perspectives and practice.* Newbury Park, CA: Sage.

Perlman, H. H. (1957). *Social casework: A problem-solving process.* Chicago: University of Chicago Press.

Perlman, H. H. (1986). The problem-solving model. In F. J. Turner (Ed.), *Social work treatment: Interlocking theoretical approaches* (3rd ed.). New York: Free Press.

President's Commission on Mental Health. (1978). *Task panel reports.* Washington, DC: U.S. Government Printing Office.

Reid, W. J., & Epstein, L. (1972). *Task centered casework.* New York: Columbia University Press.

Ryan, C. R. (1991). Where do we go from here? *Social Work, 36* (1), 3–4.

Turner, F. J. (1986). Psychosocial treatment. In F. J. Turner (Ed.), *Social work treatment: Interlocking theoretical approaches* (3rd ed.). New York: Free Press.

Turner, J. C., & Ten Hoor, W. J. (1978). The NIMH community support program: Pilot approach to a needed social reform. *Schizophrenia Bulletin, 4,* 319–348.

Wolcott, D. L., Namir, S., Fawzy, F. I., Gottlieb, M. S., & Mitsuyasu, R. T. (1986). Illness concerns, attitudes toward homosexuality and social support in gay men with AIDS. *General Hospital Psychiatry, 8,* 395–403.

Yalom, I. (1985). *The theory and practice of group psychotherapy* (3rd ed.). New York: Basic Books.

Yamatani, H., Maguire, L., Rogers, R., & Martz, P. (in press). The effects of socioeconomic change on families. In J. Cunningham & P. Martz (Eds.). *Family matters.* Pittsburgh: University of Pittsburgh Press.

Index

A

Acquired immunodeficiency syndrome (AIDS). **See** AIDS
Adolescence
  case example of social support during, 133–137
  characteristics of, 131–133
  social support systems during, 132–133
Adulthood
  case example of social support during, 143–145
  social support systems during, 138–143
Affectionateness, 73–74
AIDS
  response of social workers to, 172
  sexual behavior and, 72, 138
  specific problems of individuals with, 172
  support systems for patients with, 172–175
Alcoholics Anonymous (AA), 32
Alcoholism, 86–90, 161
Assessment stage
  for depressed individuals, 59–60
  explanation of, 34–35
Attractiveness, power and, 77

B

Behavior modification/cognitive therapy, 22–24
Black Americans, 12

C

Cancer self–help groups, xx
Case management
  description of, 27–29, 30–31
  system development, 27
  system development stages used in, 38
  used to work with polarized families, 103
Child care
  effects on infants, 108
  responsibility for, 113, 140
Childhood
  case example of social support during, 129–131
  developmental stages of, 125–129
  social support systems during, 129
Children
  effect on marriage of, 101–102
  effects of child care on, 108
  ethnic and cultural variations regarding relationships with, 114

modeling of parent's behavior by, 128
Churches, as social support resource, 109–110
Clarification stage
for depressed individuals, 60
explanation of, 35–36
Clergy, as social support resource, 109–110
Clinical psychology, 12
Coalition development, 166
Codependent marriage
case study of, 87–90
description of, 86–87
pattern development in, 94
Commission on Families, National Association of Social Workers (NASW), 100, 121
Community organizations, 110
Conformity
in adolescents, 131–133
group pressure for, 75–76
Coping methods, within families, 102–103, 109
Cultural differences in coping methods, 102–103

D

Deinstitutionalization programs, 158–160
Depressed individuals
case examples of, 57–59, 64–66
development of support system for, 59–64, 66–68
prevalence of, 161

Depression
in AIDS patients, 172
effects of, 61
in elderly, 147
reactive, 67
as social support problem, 51, 54, 55
in women, 73–76, 140
Descartes, René, 10, 13
Diagnoses, validity and reliability of, 77–78
Diagnostic and Statistical Manual of Mental Disorders, 3rd Edition (American Psychiatric Association), 4, 78
Diagramming, used in social network analysis, 6–10, 139
Disease, social support systems and, 13–14
Divorce
and changes in family support systems, 116–117, 140–142
dimensions to address in, 95
Drug abuse, 86–87, 161
Dualism, 10, 13–14
Dysthymia, 68

E

Ecological approach to social work, 157
Economic change, 16–17
Education, role of families in, 108–109
Elderly individuals
case example of social support for, 147–150

social support systems for, 147–148
variations among, 147–148
Empirical base, 23–26
Erickson, Erik, 125, 126
Expectations, unrealistic, 40
Extended families, 111
Extended families, role of. **See** Families

F
Families
changes in structure of contemporary, 99, 111–112
extended, 111
NASW support principles for, 121–122
need for balance and mutual respect in, 113–114
patterns of coping within, 102–103, 109
role of, 98–100
Family support principles, 100, 121–122
Family support systems
for AIDS patients, 173
assistance in functioning of, 100, 108–111
case studies of, 103–107, 118–120
divorce and changes in, 116–117
for elderly family members, 146
for families with children, 138–140

and life–stage transitions, 114–116
Fathers, as role models, 83
Feedback, from social support systems, xviii
Financial resources, 40, 41
Friendships, balance within, 113
Functionalist approach to social work, 157
G
Garrett, Annette, 157
Gender issues
in adolescence, 133
case studies of marriage and, 78–82, 85–86, 87–90, 92–94
within marriage, 73–75
in single males and females, 139–140

H
Hamilton, Gordon, 157
Happiness measures, 15
Health. **See** Mental health; Physical health
Hollis, Florence, 12, 31, 154, 157
Homelessness, case study of 169–171
Homosexuals
adolescent, 133
impact of AIDS on, 72
long-term relationships of, 71–72
social systems for, 138
Human condition, 42

Human immunodeficiency virus
(HIV), 171. **See also** AIDS

I
Incidence rates, 77
Income, gender differences
   in, 140
Infancy, 125–126. **See also**
   Childhood; Children
Intervention. **See** Social support
   system intervention

L
Libby, Betsy, 157
Life crises, adult, 142
Life stages
   adolescence as, 131–137
   adulthood as, 137–146
   childhood as, 125–131
   family support systems and,
      114–116, 151
   old age as, 146–151
Litwin, H., 147–148

M
Marital work approach
   defining problem as, 84–86
   determining what works in,
      91–94
   determining who has problem
      as, 86–90
   improving situation as, 90–91
Marriage
   case studies of gender
      differences and, 78–82,
      92–94

codependent, 86–92
   effect of children on, 101–102
   gender, roles, and expectations
      of, 16, 72–75
   mental health of men and
      women and, 72
   nontraditional variations in,
      71–72
   social support systems in, 139
Medications, antidepression, 68
Men
   effects of marriage on, 16, 72
   relative rates of mental illness
      among, 75–77
   role within marriage of, 72–75
Mental health
   development of definition of,
      10–14
   effect of social support on,
      3–4
   family and, 98–100
   meaning of, 4–5
Mental illness
   among men and women,
      75–77
   issue of relative rates of,
      77–78
   long-term care for, 159–164
Mentally ill patients
   continuum of services for,
      160–161
   deinstitutionalization programs
      for, 159, 160
   treatment of, 10–11
Midlife crises, 142

N

Narcissistic individuals, 56

National Association of
Social Workers
family support principles of,
100, 121–122
role in poverty-related
issues, 166

National Center for Social Policy
and Practice, 167

Need, individuality of, 52,
54–55

Neighborhood, role in family
support, 100

Network diagramming, used in
social network analysis,
6–10, 140

Network intervention. **See**
Social network analysis;
Social networks
explanation of, 27–28
stages of, 29–30
system development stages
used in, 38
used to work with
polarized families, 103

Neurosis, gender differences in
rate of, 75

O

Oglala Sioux, 1–2

P

PACE (Political Action for
Candidate Election), 166

Parataxic distortion, 51, 53–54

Parenthood
effect on marriage, 101–102
skills of, 128

Perceptions of reality, 51–53

Perlman, Helen Harris, 12,
155–157

Personal Networking
Assessment Instrument, 6, 7

Personality disorders, 75, 161

Physical health, in elderly,
147, 148

Physical problems, 39

Piaget, Jean, 126

Pine Ridge Indian Reservation,
1–2

Planning stage
for depressed individuals, 60
explanation of, 36–37

Political climate, 40–41

Poverty
effects of, 164
among elderly, 148
homelessness and, 169–171
macro orientation to, 164–167
micro orientation to, 168–169

Power, attractiveness and, 76

President's Commission of
Mental Health, 25

Prestige, in adolescence,
133–134

Prevalence rates, 77

Program coordination, 40

Psychiatry, changes in field
of, 12

Psychodynamic/ego psychology,
as intervention approach, 22–24

Psychosocial approach to social
work, 157–158

R

Rankian approach to social
work, 157
Reality, faulty perceptions of,
51–53
Reid, W. J., 154, 155
Rejection, group pressure
and, 76
Religious institutions, as social
support resource, 109–110
Respect, within families,
113–114
Restructuring stage
for depressed individuals,
60–61
explanation of, 37
Retirement, 147–148
Reynolds, Bertha, 157
Richmond, Mary, 157
Rogers, Carl, 4
Role models, fathers as, 83

S

Schedule of Recent
Experiences, 15
Schizophrenia
etiology of, 99
rate of, 75, 161
Schizophrenics
case study of, 162–164
social support systems for, 26
Self-esteem

effect of depression on, 61
problem of poor, 51, 53–54
Self-help groups
for AIDS patients, 174–175
as aspect of system
development, 31–33
benefits of, xix–xx
for divorced people, 141
for families, 110–111
for single parents, 141
view of social workers by, 32
Self, sense of, xvii–xviii
Separateness, balancing support
and, 42–45
Sexual behavior, impact of AIDS
on, 72
Sexually transmitted diseases,
72, 138
Single parents
impact of children on, 114
self-help groups for, 141
social life of, 141
Sioux, 1–2
Social network analysis
diagramming used for,
6–10, 139
questionning used for, 9–10
studies in, 3
Social networks
explanation of, 2–3
and life-stage transitions,
114–115
types of, 22
Social skills
problem of deficient, 52,
55–57

promotion of, xx–xxi
Social support
  analyzing, 2–5
  effect on mental health, 3–4
  need for, xvi
  research and epidemiological
    studies on, 14–17
  resources provided by,
    xvii–xxi
Social support intervention
  candidates for, 39
  problems and limitations of,
    39–41
  program coordination for, 40
  rationale for using, 41–42
Social support problems
  deficient social skills, 52,
    55–57
  depression, 51, 54, 55
  faulty perceptions of reality,
    51–53
  individuality of need,
    52, 54–55
  parataxic distortion and poor
    self-esteem, 51, 53–54
Social support system
    intervention
  approaches to, 22–26
  background of, 21–22
  types, 26–33
Social support system model,
    22–23
Social support systems
  changes in contemporary,
    11–13
  coalition development and, 167

defining client's, 5–10
divorce and changes in,
    116–117
explanation of, xv, 2, 3
for families, 100, 108–111. **See
    also** Families
formal vs. informal, 45–46
future applications of,
    158–163
past and present applications
    of,154–158
purpose and application of,
    xv, xvi
Social work
  psychosocial approach to,
    157–158
  varying approaches to, 12, 31,
    155–158
Social workers, xv–xvi
Status, in adolescence,
    132–133
Stress
  in contemporary family, 109
  familial responsibilities of
    women and, 74–75
  related to divorce, 95
  resulting from changing
    support systems, 115
  social support as protection
    against, xviii–xix, 14–16
Suicide, in adolescence,
    131–132
Supporting theory, 23–25
Synagogues, as social support
    resource, 109–110
System development

case management vs., 27
description of, 31–33
explanation of, 27, 28
used to work with polarized
    families, 103
System development stages, 33
    assessment as, 34–35
    clarification as, 35–36
    planning as, 36–37
    restructuring as, 37
    usefulness as, 38
    ventilation as, 34
Systems theory, 25

T
Training requirements, for social
    support intervention, 40
Treatment model, 23–26

U
Unemployed individuals, 32–33

Unemployment
    gender differences in, 140
    study of effects of, 16–17
Usefulness of stages, 38

V
Value premises, 23, 24, 26
Ventilation stage
    for depressed individuals, 59
    explanation of, 34
Viruses, ability to withstand
    effects of, 14

W
Weber, Max, 42
Women
    depression in, 73–77
    earning power of, 112
    effects of marriage on, 16, 72
    relative rates of mental illness
        among, 75–77
    working outside of home, 112

About the Author

Lambert Maguire, PhD, ACSW, has more than 20 years of clinical practice experience in private practice, community mental health centers, hospitals, and residential treatment centers, and as a commissioned officer in the U.S. Public Health Service on the Pine Ridge Reservation. He has a joint doctorate in social work and psychology from the University of Michigan and is a graduate of the University of Chicago's School of Social Service Administration and Loyola University in Chicago.

Since 1978 he has been on the faculty of the University of Pittsburgh's School of Social Work where he chairs the clinical area in the MSW program. He has been the principal investigator for several National Institute of Mental Health projects dealing with networks and social support systems in clinical practice, and he teaches practice courses to master's- and doctoral-level students in social work.